"In a world where perfection reigns supreme, the encouraging words found within these pages contain a message of hope and inspiration. *Home Made Lovely* is all about the importance of celebrating the everyday, taking small steps toward a bigger change, and understanding the importance of loving your home right where it's at. This book is what we've all been looking for—a simple road map to creating a more peaceful and beautiful home."

—KARIANNE WOOD, owner, Thistlewood Farms

"Shannon's *Home Made Lovely* touches upon one of the most important aspects when creating a beautiful home, and that is the importance of decorating your home with the center focus being family, friends, and hospitality. Shannon does a wonderful job breaking down the basic decorating do's and don'ts in layman's terms."

—LUCY AKINS, Craftberry Bush

"Shannon paints a beautiful picture of the purpose behind creating a lovely home. Her practical advice made me realize a home doesn't have to be perfectly styled, expensive, or redone with every trend to be a cozy, happy refuge for the people I love most!"

—LISA BASS, author of *Simple Farmhouse Life*

"I loved reading Shannon's book, *Home Made Lovely*. Shannon shares easy ways to create YOUR perfect home! Shannon's book is full of wonderful tips on how to find your style and declutter your home, as well as guides for coordinating colors and patterns as you decorate, and so much more!"

—JENNIFER HADFIELD, Tatertots and Jello

"I've been following Shannon's blog for years and enjoy her honest approach to decorating for your family and within your budget. There are so many fresh new tips in this book that I can't wait to implement in my home!"

—JANET COON, author/designer, Shabbyfufu

"Shannon's realistic perspective on creating a home is a breath of fresh air to the posh world of glossy magazine perfection. From evaluating the heart of the matter to being intentional with our spaces, this book is a trustworthy friend holding your hand to help you conquer it all, one room at a time. You're going to love this one-of-a-kind guide to making a home truly lovely."

—ASHLEY MILLS, The Handmade Home

"Not only does this book offer practical advice on home decorating, it's full of encouragement and inspiration beyond decor. I was challenged and moved after I read Shannon's words about blessing our home and hospitality. It's a must-read for anyone who wants to make their home feel welcoming and special!"

—CHRISTINA DENNIS, The DIY Mommy

"In *Home Made Lovely*, Shannon does a beautiful job of weaving together valuable tips and ideas for the home, personal stories and illustrations, and encouragement and inspiration to give readers the confidence and knowledge they need to create a home they love, no matter where they live."

—ABBY LAWSON, author, creator of Just a Girl and Her Blog and Abby Organizes

"No wonder Shannon's book is called *Home Made Lovely*! Shannon has crafted a home that is filled with a sense of comfort and loveliness! And she so generously shares her God-centered attitude and tons of amazing tips to help us create a home that is lovely too! Beautiful read!"

—YVONNE PRATT, StoneGable

"Our homes are our soft place to land. I love that Shannon not only teaches HOW to decorate, but shares with us WHY. This book will inspire you to make your home your own, give you the confidence to decorate like a pro, and give you tips to stay within your budget."

—STACY RISENMAY author of *Natural Accents*

"I love how Shannon makes having a home to love so simple! From practicing gratitude, organizing, and decorating to easy entertaining tips, this is a go-to guide to creating a lovely home!"

—JENNIFER RIZZO, lifestyle blogger, author of *Creatively Christmas*

"Shannon is down-to-earth and enchants the reader with a godly insight into hospitality and the home. From decluttering and decorating tips to recipes and DIYs, you'll be inspired to decorate, entertain, and bless those around you."

—KELLY S. ROWE, author, creator of Live Laugh Rowe

"*Home Made Lovely* was not only educational, but extremely inspiring! Making a house a home is an art, and Shannon is the master artist! There were many topics she touched on that don't come natural to me, like hospitality, and reading her tips helped me feel I could be successful at making others feel welcome in my home. This beautiful book is going to be a treasure and wonderful resource for me as I strive to make my own home lovely."

—CAMI GRAHAM, creator of TIDBITS blog and TIDBITS Planners, www.tidbits-cami.com and www.tidbitsplanners.com

"Shannon completely demystified the decorating process not once, but twice for me in this book. As a long-time home blogger, I think about decor and hospitality quite a bit, but she clarified these things for me in a way that opened my eyes to a simpler way of doing things."

—COURTENAY HARTFORD, owner, The Creek Line House

"Shannon is one of the most natural and gifted teachers I've ever known. Her attitude toward loving the home you have and making it as lovely as possible—and then opening it up to your family and friends—will leave you feeling inspired, equipped, and hopeful."

—DANNYELLE NICOLLE-RAMJIST, Life Is a Party

HOME
MADE LOVELY

HOME
MADE LOVELY

Creating the Home You've Always Wanted

SHANNON ACHESON

BETHANYHOUSE
a division of Baker Publishing Group
Minneapolis, Minnesota

© 2020 by Shannon Acheson

Published by Bethany House Publishers
11400 Hampshire Avenue South
Bloomington, Minnesota 55438
www.bethanyhouse.com

Bethany House Publishers is a division of
Baker Publishing Group, Grand Rapids, Michigan

Printed in China

ISBN 978-0-7642-3537-5

Library of Congress Control Number: 2020931614

Unless otherwise indicated, Scripture quotations are from THE HOLY BIBLE, NEW INTERNATIONAL VERSION®, NIV® Copyright © 1973, 1978, 1984, 2011 by Biblica, Inc.® Used by permission. All rights reserved worldwide.

Scripture quotations labeled ESV are from The Holy Bible, English Standard Version® (ESV®), copyright © 2001 by Crossway, a publishing ministry of Good News Publishers. Used by permission. All rights reserved. ESV Text Edition: 2016

Scripture quotations labeled KJV are from the King James Version of the Bible.

Scripture quotations labeled NASB are from the New American Standard Bible® (NASB), copyright © 1960, 1962, 1963, 1968, 1971, 1972, 1973, 1975, 1977, 1995 by The Lockman Foundation. Used by permission. www.Lockman.org

Scripture quotations labeled NKJV are from the New King James Version®. Copyright © 1982 by Thomas Nelson. Used by permission. All rights reserved.

Scripture quotations labeled TLV are from the Tree of Life Version. © 2015 by the Messianic Jewish Family Bible Society. Used by permission of the Messianic Jewish Family Bible Society.

Photos on pages 14, 38, 53–66, 70, 139, 146, 162–4, 170–2, 174, 177–9, and 182–4 by Shannon Acheson

Cover design by Dan Pitts
Interior design by William Overbeeke
Illustrations on pages 73–6, 131, 134, and 137 by Jennifer Horton

Author represented by William K. Jensen Literary Agency

20 21 22 23 24 25 26   7 6 5 4 3 2

To Dean, Jonah, Lillian, and Megan.
Home is wherever I'm with you.

CONTENTS

INTRODUCTION

I LOVE A PRETTY HOME, DON'T you? It's something I've always loved—even as a teenager living in my parents' house. Like most women, I'm most at peace in a home that is well-organized, beautiful, and clutter-free. I also love to decorate and fluff and move things around to create lovelier spaces.

I've learned that we decorate our homes for all sorts of reasons. Some of us do it to impress the neighbors and keep up with the Joneses (whoever they are). Some of us decorate to fill a void of some sort. And some of us decorate because we want to bring both beauty and meaning into our homes. That last group is who this book is for . . . women like you and me who want our homes to be beautiful while making our families, friends, and neighbors feel like the one-of-a-kind, genuinely loved, special creations they are. Home is our happy place. Or at least that's what we want it to be.

I also know that we often don't know where to start or how to put it all together.

If you're like me, you may have pretended that decorating your home isn't that important, even though you'd like nothing more. And you might be sick and tired of spending time and money on decorating, only to have your home look no better than it did before. And all of that can feel very overwhelming.

I've written *Home Made Lovely* partly as a decorating book. But it's not *just* a decorating book. Yes, I'm going to show you how to declutter and organize all the things in just seven simple steps so that you can function well in your home. And I'm going to walk you through the process I use to decorate every single room in my house *on a budget* in simple, repeatable steps that you can use too—even if you have no idea what you're doing when you pick up this book. I'm also going to talk to you about hospitality and loving on your friends and neighbors.

Home Made Lovely is different than other decorating books because I believe that decorating our homes should be about those that reside inside them, not creating a magazine-worthy spread. That before we decorate anything, we should first consider ourselves, our family, and our heavenly Father. I believe that creating a peaceful and welcoming home begins by clarifying who you're decorating for, being thankful for the home you have in this season, and *deliberately dedicating it to God.*

With that foundation in place we can do all those other things I talked about. We can choose a style, create a whole home decorating plan, and make it look pretty and welcoming. All without the overwhelm.

Throughout these pages, I'm going to show you how to:

- decorate in a way that suits your family's *real life*
- do a house blessing and dedicate your home to God
- practice being thankful for the home you have in your current life season
- declutter and organize everything before you decorate, and/or whenever it's needed again
- decorate your whole home step-by-step, in the correct order, one room at a time (as your time and budget allow)

Plus, I am going to share more than twenty simple hospitality ideas to make your own family, as well as guests, feel welcome and loved in your home. You know, just to get you going.

I personally know (and hear from my readers and email subscribers all the time) how hard it is to keep a house organized when you have kids coming and going. How difficult it is to figure out your decorating style and how to pull your whole house together into one lovely, cohesive look.

If you're like most women, you want a "home made lovely" but you have no clue where to start. And on top of it, you don't want to get so concerned about the paint colors that you forget about the people. My job is to help you keep the main thing the main thing.

When you finish this book, you may wonder, *Will I have a more beautiful, organized home?* The answer is unequivocally yes!

But do you know what else you'll have? Your sanity. The peace God intended for you to have. Money left in your bank account. And, if you live under a roof with other people, you'll also have people who won't resent you but will embrace these changes right along with you.

So, let's get started, shall we?

PART 1

WHO ARE YOU DOING IT ALL FOR?

CHAPTER 1

The Most Important Place on Earth

GIVEN THAT I AM AN INTER-ior decorator, and for the last nine-plus years have written a blog mainly about decorating, it shouldn't be a surprise that my first traditionally published book is about decorating and home. It is what I know, after all. And "they" say you should always write what you know. But, as I mentioned in the introduction, this isn't *just* a decorating book.

While I'm quite used to writing step-by-step tutorials and how-to articles about organizing a home in five steps or choosing the right paint color on my blog, I find it a little harder to write about the why behind those things. Maybe because the why isn't easily boiled down into a step-by-step process or a particular number of

points. Maybe it's because I'm a teacher at heart, and I love to take big ideas and simplify them into actionable steps. It's kind of my superpower. It just feels oh-so-much more difficult to articulate what, or rather who, truly matters in a home and what that means for decorating, than it does to write "8 Steps to Make Your Home Look More Stylish on a Budget." (Which is actually the title of one of my most popular blog posts.)

But, as I've gotten older, I've come to really understand that it's the people— your family and mine, plus our friends and neighbors—who are the most important in our homes, with all the how-to's and decorating built around their collective wants and needs.

So, here goes.

What's So Special about Home, Anyway?

I've always believed that home is an incredibly special place. Sacred ground even, if that's not sacrilegious. I mean, think about it. Where do you most want to be after a long trip? *Home, in your own bed.* Why are grown men and women so sad when their parents sell their childhood home? *Because it's still home even after they've left it to create a home of their own.* Where do we all start from, at least according to T. S. Eliot? *Home.* Where did E.T. want to phone? *Home.* Okay, that last one is from a fictional story. But it still illustrates that even moviemakers and scriptwriters believe that home matters.

Home is our happy place—the most important place on earth, which is, coincidentally, the title of a book I read when our kids were babies.[2] It taught me early on in my adult life that home is about the people who live there.

It shaped much of what I fundamentally believe about home and how we should live there, *especially as Christians.*

My Home Story

Even though I mainly write step-by-step and how-to articles, I'm a heart-on-my-sleeve girl. I'm a romantic through and

through and just can't help it. I fall for all of those cheesy romantic comedy, girl-meets-boy storylines—hook, line, and sinker. Every. Single. Time. Seriously, those Hallmark Channel movies are my favorite. Fortunately, God took pity on my romantic, sappy heart and brought my husband, Dean, and I together at a young age (I was nineteen and he was twenty-three) and has blessed us with a very good marriage. That doesn't mean it's perfect. It doesn't mean we agree on everything or never argue. It just means we've learned how to lean in and live peacefully together, still very much in love with each other after three kids, eleven homes, and twenty-three-plus years of marriage. (And, if you can add, you now know how old we are. *Moving on.*)

When Dean and I got together all those years ago, we had both already been through a lot in our separate young lives. Once we were married, we both knew we wanted a different kind of home life than a lot of other homes we knew of. We vowed never to go to bed angry and never to talk about each other behind the other's back. We agreed that name calling was never allowed in our house and that we would stay together no matter what. It became my goal to make our home as peaceful and lovely as possible, at least in part through decorating.

Listen, my friend, life is crazy. You and I both know this. We move at a frenetic pace from one appointment to the next

> *"Home is where one starts from."*[1]
>
> *T. S. Eliot*

and barely have time to sit down to a meal together with those we love (more on this later). This busyness is exactly the reason we need to create a peaceful, restful home. To give ourselves, our families, and our friends somewhere to just be still.

> According to a survey published in *A Journal of the Association for Psychological Science*, certain rooms can produce very tangible emotions. The 200 participants of the research were given a list of hypothetical rooms typical for an average home, and asked to choose two ambiance descriptions of each of them. Unsurprisingly, the results matched what is the conventional wisdom of interior design, e.g., the entry room should be inviting, the master bedroom reflects a sense of romance, the closet represents organization, etc.[3]

Interior surroundings have the ability to evoke either a negative or positive emotional response. Everything from colors, to natural elements, to ceiling height and lighting affects how we feel when we walk into a room. Our homes can be molded and shaped in a way that promotes good mood and even health.

"The ache for home lives in all of us, the safe place where we can go as we are and not be questioned."

Maya Angelou

Be still, and know that I am God. (Psalm 46:10)

The right kind of decor can create a peacefulness. We know this is true when we walk into a certain home, and even if everything isn't perfectly tidy, there's a homey peacefulness to it. We know it when we walk into certain restaurants, dimly lit with candles on every table. The way a room looks and feels settles into our spirits and can calm even the most anxious heart.

It's because of all this that I love a pretty home. My mother and I used to visit model homes just for fun on weekends and dream of the life we could live in those beautifully, if not sparsely, decorated spaces. Dean and I still do this sometimes for a different perspective and for new ideas for our own home. I mean, where else can you go to wander through an entire house that's been decorated from top to bottom? The main floor panel molding we installed in our current house, for example, was inspired by model homes we visited shortly before we moved to our home near Toronto. I thrive in spaces that are well organized and beautiful. I'm guessing you're the same, whether you're consciously aware of it or not. But I also know that a truly lovely and beautiful home should be about so much more than just how it looks.

So, Who Are You Decorating Your Home For?

An acquaintance recently told me a story. She worked as a decorator for several years. In that time, she worked with rather wealthy clients who could afford pretty much whatever decor they wanted. She told me about one particular married couple whom she worked with; their story shares a common theme with many I've heard from other designers and decorators. This wife dragged her husband to one decor consult after another and through shop after shop to look at paint and wall coverings, rugs and furniture. Truthfully, though, the husband really didn't care which things his wife chose, or even how much money she spent to decorate their home. Do you know what he did want? At the end of the day, he simply wanted a comfortable chair to sit in. That's all. Sadly, his wife didn't allow this one thing in their "designer" house, because it didn't fit the *look* she was going for!

And that's the heart of it, right there. She was not decorating for him at all. Who was she decorating her home for? Was it for the neighbors? Her friends? For bragging rights? To get featured on TV or in a magazine? There's no way for us, as outsiders, to know for sure. But it certainly wasn't for her husband or their family. Which again begs the question, Who are you and I decorating our homes for?

Because I write about decor all the time and am constantly looking at photos of pretty spaces, I find it very easy to get caught up in what everyone else is doing, how they're decorating, what's new, and what's popular. Which is okay, if I truly like

Home should make "you feel like a valued 'customer' the moment you walk through the front door . . . a safe place where you can make mistakes."[4]

those things. But in this brave new world of Pinterest and Instagram, it's oh-so-easy for you and I both to feel like we *should* be decorating our home a certain way, depending on the trend of the moment, whether it works for our homes and families or not. (We'll talk more about trends later in chapter 5.) It's so easy to fall into the comparison trap, thinking our homes are somehow "less than" if we don't have the same things or decorate the same way as all those "influencers." (I *really* don't like that word!)

So, who are we decorating for?

The short answer for me has *always* been, for the people who live in my home with me. Of course, there's consideration taken for the guests and extended family who visit (which we'll talk about later too, in chapters 10 and 11). And because it's part of our business, I've often thought of the blog in the decor decision-making process too. But mainly, I decorate for our family of five, plus one little doggie, because we live in this space three hundred and sixty-five days a year. Because our kids are homeschooled and I work from home, we quite literally spend more time here than anywhere else. But even if I worked somewhere else and our kids left each day for school, I would be decorating for my family first and foremost. Because this is our *home*.

What has this looked like over the years? Well, when our kids were little, decorating for our family meant that lower cabinets and drawers were filled with the kids' toys and books, and my pretty things were carefully placed up and out of the reach of tiny hands. It meant we had a black leather sofa for years, simply because it blended into the decor and was the easiest thing to clean juice, puke, and kids' boogers off of! (All you parents know what I'm talking about!) We deliberately kept furniture and decor sparse for a period of time to make room for all the baby and toddler things that seemed to daily multiply like rabbits (and only came in bright, shiny primary colors when my kids were small).

These days, decorating for our family means that we Scotchgard our upholstered dining room chairs because we want to be comfortable, but teenagers live here. (Plus, I'm a klutz and am more likely to spill something than they are.) It means the kids have always had a say in choosing their bedroom colors because their rooms are their space, even though the control freak in me *really* wanted to just choose them myself. It means I carefully arrange throw pillows on the couch and our bed because I adore how it looks, but often put them away for everyday use so Dean doesn't have to move them all just to sit down. It means we have white trim and doors that frequently get wiped clean with Mr. Clean Magic Erasers and touched up with fresh paint because white trim makes me happy. It means our basement is more colorful than our main floor because it's a space where our teenagers and their friends hang out. I decorate for *us*.

The biggest thing I took away from *The Most Important Place on Earth* was that *home should make people feel special.* It's almost absurd in its simplicity.

What do I mean by *special*? Well, like how special you feel when your crazy dog welcomes you home. You know what I'm saying. Whether you're gone for a week's holiday or you step out to the garage for two minutes to take the garbage out, your dog is *always* so insanely happy to see you that he wiggles his bum and wags his tail so hard he almost falls over. Like you're the most important person on earth. *That's the kind of special I'm referring to.* Your home should make you and your family feel that way too.

We can choose to *only* make our house pretty to look at. Stylish. On-trend. Filled with the things some (likely very talented) designer says we should have . . . all while making our family feel like an afterthought. But I believe that the purpose of creating a beautiful home is not so we can step back

> "A man travels the world over in search of what he needs and returns home to find it."
>
> *George A. Moore*

and say, "Look how gorgeous my house is," like the wife from the comfy chair story. Instead, I believe we should decorate with our family as our first thought, in such a way that they feel as special as they should. After all, we are created in God's image, and He is the Creator of beautiful things. He gives us all sorts of things in nature to bring peacefulness and joy to our lives—sunrises and sunsets, oceans, beaches, and forests. He also gives each of us the ability to create havens of love and joy inside the walls of our home. He doesn't demand perfection or magazine-ready designs. He doesn't expect us to be "on-trend." Not at all. But He does give us the command to love one another as He has loved us (John 13:34–35). For me, a comfortable home is one tangible way to love the people within it. It's a way to say, "Come home. You belong here."

And choosing to decorate with this front of mind, my friend, is the first step in creating a "home made lovely."

CHAPTER 2

Practice an (Ongoing) Attitude of Gratitude

OKAY, SO YOU'RE ON BOARD with making your home your happy place and you understand the importance of your home environment to your family. But what if you don't love the home you happen to have in this season? What if it's in the wrong neighborhood? Or it doesn't look like the farmhouse home you've imagined in your head? What if it's a rental or military housing? Well, here's the truth . . .

There is no perfect home. There really isn't. No matter what lotteries or HGTV call their dream homes. No matter whether you've built your own home or moved into a little fixer-upper. There just aren't any one-hundred-percent-perfect homes this side of heaven. Winners renovate HGTV and lottery dream homes to suit *their* family better. People who have built

their own homes find imperfections after they actually move in. And fixer-uppers are, well, full of surprises!

But there is *the home that you have right now.* The one that God has provided for you *in this season.* And you and I both can learn to truly love our homes in spite of all their imperfections. We can learn to see through new eyes and make the most of where we live *right now.*

I'm a dreamer. I look at ALL spaces and see them for what they one day *could be.* A little paint here and a little laminate there and things take shape in my imagination. I can dream up all sorts of fixes and improvements. When I see an imperfect house with my eyes, I see it as its best self in my imagination.

But I'm also a realist. I know that where I am right now—at any point in my life—

needs to be enjoyed or at the very least appreciated. Even if that's not yet what my imagination pictures.

Take our past homes, for example. Dean and I have lived in eleven different places in our twenty-three-plus years of marriage. Everything from one-bedroom basement apartments we lived in when I was in college to the 2,000-square-foot, two-story home that we now share with our teenagers. I can truthfully say that I appreciated all of them. Have some been nicer than others? Absolutely! Did I love every inch of all of them? No, of course not. Was I thankful for each one while we lived there? Yes, I was!

One of my favorite places was actually one of the most run down, tiny, and broken old houses anyone has ever seen. It was the sort of house I imagine the old country song "Little Houses"[1] was written about.

You see, Dean and I were in a season of exhaustion and brokenness when that house became ours. We had run ourselves into the ground financially, physically, and emotionally. Dean had commuted almost two hours each way to work for five years, burning out three cars in the process. We had three young children, and we had served in our beloved church nonstop for the same five years. We needed a change, we needed a break, and we needed to be closer to Dean's work in the city. That little white house was all we could afford . . . and she needed some serious TLC.

Our little white house originally had only two bedrooms and one small bath-room. The hot water tank and washer and dryer were in the kitchen. Like *in* the kitchen. There was an air conditioner sticking out a hole in the side wall. And the house had a dirt floor crawl space that Dean had to army crawl through in a hazmat-style suit just to change the furnace filter! Our friends thought we were absolutely insane to buy that house, though no one said so until years later. (I'm not sure whether that's a good thing or a bad thing.)

Through the grace of God (and the faith of some of our family that we would be able to pay them back), we were able to borrow enough money to fix up the worst part of the house, the kitchen. And through the kindness and guidance of some friends who at the time were much more experienced with renos than Dean and I, we renovated that little seven-by-fourteen-foot kitchen and laundry room combination in a month. It turned out to be a fabulous little space, packed with the function and organization of a much larger kitchen.

About a year later, the back roof in that tiny house had a massive leak caused by ice damming. It was a horrible thing to wake up to and I was honestly heartbroken. After all the hard work in the adjacent kitchen, the dining room ceiling was bulging with water. It was pouring from the light fixture. The floor was sopping wet. We were still recuperating emotionally and financially from our previous stretching season. We were terrified of what the damage would cost us. But the horrible mess turned into a blessing just a few hours later when we realized that ice damming was covered by our homeowners' insurance. Hallelujah! By doing the repairs ourselves, with the insurance money we were able to fix up the dining room and living room years before our own budget would have allowed us to.

And that little house. Oh, that little house. It became the place Dean and I discovered we could work together. That we could dream and create beautiful things as a team. Our business, Home Made Lovely, was essentially born there. It was where our kids learned to ride their bikes and walk to the park for the first time on their own. It was where we met with our then-new small group and began to grow with our now best friends. And when our family of five outgrew those nine hundred and fifty square feet after three years, I was honestly sad to say goodbye to our little white house.

You see, when we lived there, I didn't focus on the tired roof or the broken floors. I didn't see how small the house was. I mean, I saw those things, but I didn't dwell on them. Instead, I focused on what could be done, how much potential the house had. How our family could use it and grow. And how I could be efficient and organized in any size space. That house did more for my design and home philosophy than any other one before or since.

If you find yourself living in a house that is less than what you'd hoped for, you don't have to be miserable. You don't have to hate it.

Of course, you can make improvements as your time and budget allow. You can follow all the steps in the rest of this book and shape your house into the home you want it to be. But if you can't make as much progress as you'd like as quickly as you'd like (we are such impatient beings!), you can still appreciate the home you have right now with a few simple steps. *I did tell you that breaking big things down into manageable steps is my superpower, right?*

How to Love the Home You Have

Believe it or not, loving the home you have is possible. Here's how to do it.

First of all, make a list of the things you like or even love about your house. You can do this in your head, but it really helps to write it down. Is your house on a great street? Does it have a great view? Maybe there's a main floor laundry room? A pretty front door? Or maybe, if it needs a lot of work and you can't see anything good about it, you can love it for the simple fact that it's a shelter from the storms of life (both literally and figuratively) for this season. Write down any and all good things about your house. Post this somewhere you will see it often.

Next, as you find yourself going about your day, when you think something negative about your house, look at your list and say something out loud that you're thankful for from the list of things you just wrote. This simple act of seeing it and speaking it out loud helps to instill it in your brain.

Finally, whenever you're praying, be sure to include a prayer of thanks to God for the things on your list. For the shelter your home provides. For the beauty that is there, even if it's invisible still. Pray something as simple as, "Dear Lord, thank you for your provision and the gift of our home. Thank you that it provides shelter and a safe place for our family to live and for friends to visit."

The more you focus on the positive things that are part of your home right now, the easier it will be to appreciate it and truly be thankful for your home without having to deliberately concentrate on the positive. Even if it's not your dream home!

LOVE THE HOME YOU HAVE

Use this space to write down all that you're thankful for about your home.

CHAPTER 3

As for Me and My House

Depending on where you are in your Christian walk, or if you're not a Christian, this chapter may seem a little strange to include in a book about decorating. Or you might be a devoted Christian who has been following Jesus for years, but as you read through this chapter, you might find that my approach doesn't follow your faith practices. That's okay too. The Bible doesn't command you to do what I'm about to describe in this chapter. But in our home, we've found this to be a way to bring peace into our environment. Even if these suggestions provide a different way of practicing faith, perhaps you will pick up an idea or two that works just right for you.

W HEN VISITING, PEOPLE have often told us how peaceful our home feels and how relaxed they are when they are here. I always smile when they say this, because I know that creating that feeling and special place of rest isn't a coincidence or accident.

It is something Dean and I have been very deliberate about, especially in the last few years.

As a decorator, I facilitate making our family and friends comfortable by making our home physically welcoming right from the moment they see our front door. I create lovely curb appeal and a welcoming entryway. I invite them to make themselves at home. (We'll talk later about how you can do that too.)

As a *Christian* and a decorator, my approach is somewhat different. Maybe *different* isn't the right word. Maybe *more than* or *in addition to* would be a better description? Here's what I'm talking about.

Whom Does Your House Belong To?

In Ephesians 6:12, the Bible tells us that "our struggle is not against flesh and blood, but against the rulers, against the authorities, against the powers of this dark world and against the spiritual forces of evil in the heavenly realms." I believe this verse to be true, that there are spiritual forces of good and evil fighting against each other. Yes, spiritual warfare is very real, even in this "enlightened" day and age. People with the spiritual gift of discernment know this very well and can often recognize that a space feels "off" because of the influence of "spiritual forces of evil." But often with or without that God-given gift someone can feel relaxed or stressed in a space too; they just aren't usually able to articulate why they feel that way.

If you live in an older home, it's very likely that families have lived there before yours. Families that maybe had entirely different beliefs than yours. Families that had all sorts of baggage and plenty of their own inherited issues. Maybe an alcoholic lived there, or a family that didn't believe in God or the Bible. Maybe someone who just happened to swear a lot lived there. Maybe a family lived there that watched horror movies, or messed around with Ouija boards or palm reading. Things that, as Christians, we know we're not supposed to do because of the power who's behind those things (hint: it's *not* your heavenly Father). Even if you live in a brand-new home, there have been many people in and out building and constructing and inspecting. That's a lot of opportunity for negative spiritual influences.

Dean and I have lived in a lot of places over the years. As I mentioned in chapter 1, we got married when we were young. I went to college after we were married. As a result, we rented many basement apartments and parts of other people's homes before we bought our first house. At that time we were not yet Christians, and I spent a lot of time worrying and being afraid in a few of those apartments. At the time, I couldn't put my finger on why I felt safe and secure at one place and scared and depressed at another. Looking back, I now know it was because of some of my own and a lot of other people's spiritual junk pressing in upon me in the homes I felt horrible in and lack thereof in the other homes.

After becoming a Christian in 2002, I began reading the Bible and studying Scripture more. In time, I came upon Joshua 24:15, now a familiar verse, which reads, in part: "As for me and my house, we will serve the LORD" (ESV). This was a slow-burn lightbulb moment for me in my home journey—kind of like those old-school energy-efficient lightbulbs that were dim when they were first turned on, but got brighter the longer they were left on.

Everything we own as Christians belongs to God. We are simply stewards or caretakers of all that we have. With that stewardship comes a choice of who we are going to serve with those possessions: ourselves, the devil, or our heavenly Father.

Truthfully, sometimes I forget and choose myself. But more often, I hope and pray that I choose God.

We have many options for dedicating our homes to God and marking them for His service. Some are mere reminders, others are bolder statements and declarations. Let's start with the reminders and then move on to the other things.

Writing Scripture on Walls and Floors

Deuteronomy 6:9 was written as an instruction for the Israelites. God tells them to remember His words and His commands, to tie them on their foreheads, and to write them on their doorframes among other things. This "doorposts" command is given again in Deuteronomy 11:13–21. All Bible verses are for edifying and teaching, but when one is repeated like this one is, we should sit up and pay extra special attention.

Now, I'm not going to tell you to write Scripture on your forehead (maybe I would if this were a beauty book instead of a decorating book!), but I *am* suggesting you write it on your house. Whether God meant for us to literally write His commands on our doorframes—as the Jewish people interpret it and do with a small scroll affixed to their front doorframes—or figuratively, the writing of Scripture on the actual constructed parts of your home is a wonderful way to dedicate it to the Lord.

So, how do you do this?

If you're building a house or renovating one, you can write Scripture verses right on the studs of your home as it's being built, starting from the front door and working your way in. You could write Scripture on subfloors before laying carpeting or tiles. If you're in a house that's already finished, as many of us are, you can write verses on the drywall or trim and then paint over them. You will know the verses are there; they just won't be visible to everyone. You can even choose different verses depending upon the room. (See the end of this chapter for a list of verses sorted by room.)

We did this in our first (purchased) home when our kids were little. As we were making over their bedrooms, we simply wrote down bold statements of faith like "You were fearfully and wonderfully made" (from Psalm 139:14) and "Be strong and courageous" (Joshua 1:6) and then painted over the verses. This was one simple way of blessing and dedicating our kids and their spaces to God.

Scripture as Art

Another way to include the Word of God in your home is to buy or create art to put on display. This is something we have done frequently over the years if we wanted to remember a particular verse or one of God's promises or even as the seasons changed. When we display Scripture art prominently where it will be seen several times a day, our minds can more readily absorb the words and recall them when we need them later.

Scripture art can be found in oh-so-many places:

- I offer several free printables on my blog, as do many of my blog friends. Simply visit HomeMade Lovely.com and search for "free printables."
- Etsy has a plethora of ready-to-frame Scripture art prints as well as downloadable printable versions to buy. Just do a Google search for "Scripture art" or "printable art" and you will find many options.
- Stores like JoAnn Fabrics, Michaels, and Hobby Lobby also have many signs, framed art prints, and other scriptural art pieces for your home.
- If you're a little bit proficient in Canva, Word, or Adobe software programs, you could make your own to print out. Staples even offers many sizes and formats for printing—including the super inexpensive, extra-large-sized black and white Engineer's print.
- I have a tutorial on the blog for how to make art of any size using a pencil transfer method if you want to paint or otherwise create your own canvases or wood signs. Visit HomeMadeLovely.com and search for "pencil transfer method."

- There are various shops online that have Scripture verses as vinyl decals too. We had one in our last home's stairwell that listed the fruit of the Spirit.
- You could even use a large chalkboard, dry-erase board, or window writing markers to write out daily or weekly verses for your family like our best friends do.

Displaying Scripture as art is a fabulous way to remember who you serve and whose child you are.

Doing a House Blessing

Another way to dedicate your house to God is to do a house blessing. A house blessing, in its simplest form, is a way of blessing our homes and dedicating them to God and His purposes. It's a way of protecting our homes from spiritual danger, much like we do by locking the doors to protect our homes and ourselves from physical danger.

You can perform a house blessing by yourself, with your husband, or with friends and family. Traditionally, in many Christian denominations, this house blessing has been performed by a minister or priest and involves lighting a candle and/or anointing the house with oil.

After going through a difficult time, when you feel the need, or after you've moved into a new home, doing a house blessing can help bring serenity and peace to your home. If you've never done a house blessing before, here's how.

1. Remove Things

Remove anything from your home that has evil roots—books, movies, posters, clothing, video games, etc. If you can't think of anything off the top of your head, pray about it and ask the Holy Spirit to show you anything that should be removed. This step is about closing doors and declaring that you don't want evil in your home in even the smallest ways.

2. Invite Close Friends and Family

Get your Christian friends and family involved in this blessing by inviting them over and having them participate. Having loved ones be a part of the blessing can add to the experience and give your loved ones a chance to bless your home as well. But if you are going to invite others, involve only those of the *same* faith and beliefs as you and your family.

3. Pray Through Each Room of Your Home

This is the core part of a house blessing and is sometimes called a prayer walk rather than a house blessing. It is the process of consecrating (making holy) your home and dedicating it as "holy ground." To do a house blessing:

a. Begin on the lowest level of your home.

b. Pray through each room, over each doorway, and around each window.

c. Continue to walk through your home, praying for each room and each space, moving up through your house. Don't forget closets, stairwells, laundry rooms, garages, and bathrooms.

d. Finish by praying over each of the four walls on the outside of your home, as well as the lowest floor and the highest ceiling (or roof). Extend this to the four sides of your property too. This is sort of like putting your home in a big protective box.

The focus of your prayers should be on the home and those who dwell in it. However, you can customize your prayers to be whatever you feel is needed. The goal of these prayers is to:

- Rebuke the devil and shut down and shut out anything that's not of God.
- Invite the Holy Spirit into your home so that He may fill it, protect it, and bless it.

Pleading the blood of Jesus Christ over each space is also very powerful. You can say something like:

"I plead the blood of Jesus Christ of Nazareth between myself/my home/

my family and the entire realm of spiritual darkness."

If someone (you or an invited family member or friend) has the spiritual gift of discernment, that can be very helpful for discerning any specific prayers that need to be prayed. For example, before we moved into our current house, we felt we needed more than just a standard prayer for it. That actually seemed a little strange at the time, because Dean and I had always done this ourselves and it really was just an average house in the suburbs, not a hundred-year-old "haunted" house. Regardless, we invited our best friends to come over and walk with Dean and me through the empty house the night before moving day, praying through each of the rooms and anointing the outer walls, windows, doors, floors, and ceilings with oil. We prayed specifically for God's presence and only His presence to be in the house. We prayed that anything left from previous owners would be removed in Jesus's name. We prayed for protection through the rooms, on the steep stairs, and in and around the pool. Fast-forward to many months later, and my finding a cassette tape of a psychic reading from the previous owner way up on a closet shelf, and our neighbors telling us that one of the previous owners always had people over with lots of screaming and weirdness that made them uncomfortable. Thankfully, we never experienced any negativity from whatever was on the tape or the people who had lived here before. And every time I walk down the stairs with my arms full of laundry, or go for a swim in the pool, I remember that we prayed about those spaces too and I don't need to worry.

4. Anoint Your Home with Oil

There is nothing mystical or magical about anointing your home with oil and it is an optional part of a house blessing. It is powerfully symbolic, though.

Anointing oil is simply oil that has been dedicated to use for God's purposes. In the Jewish faith, it is oil mixed with myrrh and cinnamon among other things. However, you can simply use olive oil that has been placed in a small vial and been prayed over, asking God to cleanse it and dedicate it to His use. Using anointing oil is a symbol of your faith and God's absolute holiness.

To anoint your home with oil, simply mark a cross on the outer walls, windows, floors, ceilings, and doorposts with the oil. Ask God to fill your home with His Holy Spirit and that every single thing that happens in your home will be *only* according to His will. This step can be done while you walk through each room praying or as a separate step at another time.

Bible Verses for Your Home

Speaking God's Word and promises back to Him is a guaranteed place of meeting

Him. It's one of the most powerful ways to pray because His Word is living and active (see Hebrews 4:12). Displaying them in your home is powerful too. If you aren't sure off the top of your head which verses you want to display in your home or use in your house blessing, here is a handy guide. I've included more than fifty verses, sorted by room and by specific need, like protection or joy. Use them as verbal prayers as you do your house blessing, write them on the very "bones" of your home, or print them out as art.

The Entryway

You will be blessed when you come in and blessed when you go out.—Deuteronomy 28:6

As for me and my house, we will serve the LORD.—Joshua 24:15 NASB

Kitchen & Dining Room

Taste and see that the LORD is good.—Psalm 34:8

Do not forget to show hospitality to strangers, for by so doing some people have shown hospitality to angels without knowing it.—Hebrews 13:2

Give us this day our daily bread.—Matthew 6:11 NKJV

They broke bread in their homes and ate together with glad and sincere hearts.—Acts 2:46

Living Room or Main Room

By wisdom a house is built, and through understanding it is established; through knowledge its rooms are filled with rare and beautiful treasures.—Proverbs 24:3–4

As for me and my house, we will serve the LORD.—Joshua 24:15 NASB

Love one another. As I have loved you, so you must love one another.—John 13:34

Unless the LORD builds the house, the builders labor in vain. Unless the LORD watches over the city, the guards stand watch in vain.—Psalm 127:1

Master Bedroom

Love is patient, love is kind. It does not envy, it does not boast, it is not proud. It does not dishonor others, it is not self-seeking, it is not easily angered, it keeps no record of wrongs. Love does not delight in evil but rejoices with the truth. It always protects, always trusts, always hopes, always perseveres.—1 Corinthians 13:4–7

We love because he first loved us.—1 John 4:19

Be completely humble and gentle; be patient, bearing with one another in love.—Ephesians 4:2

I am my beloved's and my beloved is mine.—Song of Solomon 6:3

I found the one my soul loves.—Song of Solomon 3:4 TLV

Two are better than one because they have a good return for their labor. For if either of them falls, the one will lift up his companion. But woe to the one who falls when there is not another to lift him up. Furthermore, if two lie down together they keep warm, but how can one be warm alone? And if one can overpower him who is alone, two can resist him. A cord of three strands is not quickly torn apart.*—Ecclesiastes 4:9–12 NASB

Children's Bedrooms

Don't let anyone look down on you because you are young, but set an example for the believers in speech, in conduct, in love, in faith and in purity.—1 Timothy 4:12

When you lie down, you will not be afraid; yes, you will lie down and your sleep will be sweet.—Proverbs 3:24 NKJV

Be strong and courageous. Do not be afraid; do not be discouraged, for the LORD your God will be with you wherever you go.—Joshua 1:9

Children, obey your parents in everything, for this pleases the Lord.—Colossians 3:20

---

*A cord of three strands refers to a married couple and Jesus Christ.

For God has not given us a spirit of fear, but of power and of love and of a sound mind.—2 Timothy 1:7 NKJV

She is clothed with strength and dignity; she can laugh at the days to come.—Proverbs 31:25

Be completely humble and gentle; be patient, bearing with one another in love.—Ephesians 4:2

Bathrooms

Your beauty should not come from outward adornment, such as elaborate hairstyles and the wearing of gold jewelry or fine clothes. Rather, it should be that of your inner self, the unfading beauty of a gentle and quiet spirit, which is of great worth in God's sight.—1 Peter 3:3–4

Charm is deceptive, and beauty is fleeting; but a woman who fears the LORD is to be praised.—Proverbs 31:30

Create in me a pure heart, O God, and renew a steadfast spirit within me.—Psalm 51:10

Laundry Room

Wash me, and I will be whiter than snow.—Psalm 51:7

Have mercy on me, O God, according to your unfailing love; according to your great compassion blot out my transgressions. Wash away all my iniquity and cleanse me from my sin.—Psalm 51:1–2

Office

Whatever you do, work at it with all your heart, as working for the Lord, not for human masters.—Colossians 3:23

"For I know the plans I have for you," declares the LORD, "plans to prosper you and not to harm you, plans to give you hope and a future."—Jeremiah 29:11

In all your ways acknowledge Him, and He shall direct your paths.—Proverbs 3:6 NKJV

Jesus looked at them and said, "With man this is impossible, but not with God; all things are possible with God."—Mark 10:27

God is within her, she will not fall.—Psalm 46:5

For Protection

Be strong and of good courage, do not fear nor be afraid of them; for the LORD your God, He is the One who goes with you. He will not leave you nor forsake you.—Deuteronomy 31:6 NKJV

God is our refuge and strength, a very present help in trouble.—Psalm 46:1 NKJV

We are hard-pressed on every side, yet not crushed; we are perplexed, but not in despair; persecuted, but not forsaken; struck down, but not destroyed.—2 Corinthians 4:8–9 NKJV

Many are the afflictions of the righteous, but the LORD delivers him out of them all.—Psalm 34:19 NKJV

Therefore submit to God. Resist the devil and he will flee from you.—James 4:7 NKJV

But the Lord is faithful, who will establish you and guard you from the evil one.—2 Thessalonians 3:3 NKJV

For Unity

Therefore a man shall leave his father and mother and be joined to his wife, and they shall become one flesh.—Genesis 2:24 NKJV

Bear with each other and forgive one another if any of you has a grievance against someone. Forgive as the Lord forgave you.—Colossians 3:13

Be devoted to one another in love. Honor one another above yourselves.—Romans 12:10

Live in harmony with one another. Do not be proud, but be willing to associate with people of low position. Do not be conceited.—Romans 12:16

For Joy

Rejoice always, pray continually, give thanks in all circumstances; for this is God's will for you in Christ Jesus.—1 Thessalonians 5:16–18

Though you have not seen him, you love him; and even though you do not see him now, you believe in him and are filled with an inexpressible and glorious joy, for you are receiving the end result of your faith, the salvation of your souls.—1 Peter 1:8–9

Praise the LORD. Blessed are those who fear the LORD, who find great delight in his commands.—Psalm 112:1

Finally, brothers and sisters, whatever is true, whatever is noble, whatever is right, whatever is pure, whatever is lovely, whatever is admirable—if anything is excellent or praiseworthy—think about such things.—Philippians 4:8

For Guidance

Show me your ways, LORD, teach me your paths. Guide me in your truth and teach me, for you are God my Savior, and my hope is in you all day long.—Psalm 25:4–5

Let the morning bring me word of your unfailing love, for I have put my trust in you. Show me the way I should go, for to you I entrust my life.—Psalm 143:8

Teach me to do your will, for you are my God; may your good Spirit lead me on level ground.—Psalm 143:10

Your word is a lamp for my feet, a light on my path.—Psalm 119:105

"For I know the plans I have for you," declares the LORD, "plans to prosper you and not to harm you, plans to give you hope and a future."—Jeremiah 29:11

Trust in the LORD with all your heart and do not lean on your own understanding. . . . And He will make your paths straight.—Proverbs 3:5–6 NASB

God's Word is powerful, and by declaring it in your home, you will be constantly reminded of His sovereignty and grace because you will be literally surrounded by His Word.

The Lord is sovereign, and He already has the victory in all things. Blessing your house or not blessing your house won't make or break your salvation. That is by the work of Jesus alone, and He doesn't need our help with it (Ephesians 2:8). But dedicating our homes to God with Scripture and asking for His holy protection and blessing over them affects how you and yours live your lives in freedom here on earth. By doing the things in this chapter, and even layering all three things together (Scripture tucked away in the walls, displayed as art, and said aloud as a house blessing), you will find that your home is more peaceful and even tangibly more comfortable than before.

So now that we know who we're doing all of this for, and who it all really belongs to, let's get ourselves organized and prepped to decorate!

PART 2

GETTING READY

CHAPTER 4

7 Steps to Declutter and Organize Everything

ORGANIZED AND CLUTTER-free spaces.

We all want them. And yet it can seem like a constant battle to get—and keep—them that way.

One of the questions I ask new email subscribers on our blog is "What are you struggling with most when it comes to your home?" Aside from budget being an issue for many, the most common answer is "too much clutter."

A decluttered and organized home is a home that feels less chaotic, at least most of the time. But oftentimes, organization can feel like as much of a burden as the clutter. When you overcomplicate the process or you get bogged down in the messy-before-it-gets-better part, you may think that you will never have an organized home. But that's simply not true. Organization should

work *for* the people in a home, not the other way around. It should be easy to get everything organized to begin with and to then put everything away quickly again when necessary.

It's especially important to declutter each space in your house *before* you try to decorate it. Otherwise, you'll be struggling with all that excess stuff as you try to choose colors and plan furniture placement. I know my brain can't handle that very well, so I'm assuming yours won't either!

With three homeschooled teenagers in the house and my working from home, our common spaces take a beating on a daily basis:

- Hello, basement, I'm looking at you. Seriously, when do kids learn to put things away and throw out their trash without being nagged?!

- I'm sure the kitchen has a mini tornado go through it every couple of hours when it's snack time . . . again. (You think toddlers are bad? Wait until they get bigger and start getting their own snacks. Yes, it's a blessing not to have to do everything for them. But the mess they make doing it themselves is oh-so-real!)

- Shoes can't possibly go *in* the closet, they have to go in front of it, right? (Picture me doing a facepalm right now. Also, why can't we put emojis in books?)

Because of all this, I'm frequently purging and tweaking our organizing systems. Over the years I've figured out a basic system to get and keep all the spaces pretty well organized. By that I mean that they can be picked up within a few minutes when company's coming or when Momma has had enough of the chaos.

"Being organized isn't about getting rid of everything you own or trying to become a different person; it's about living the way you want to live, but better."[1] Want to know the surefire way to get rid of clutter? The answer is to go through one space at a time and get it organized using the seven-step method I am going to outline on the next few pages. Then move on to the next space and the next. Before you know it, your whole house will be one magnificently organized beauty! It will need reorganizing occasionally. But it will be so much easier after this.

7 Steps to a Clutter-Free, Organized Home

So, how do you organize any space? It's pretty simple actually. Here are the seven steps I use to organize every space in our house:

1. Empty and Sort

Remove everything from the space you're trying to organize. Dump it all out. Create a huge pile if necessary. Then start sorting. Place like with like. Don't try to be tidy with this. The mess actually has to get worse before it can get better. Really. Just create piles of similar things. And keep going. Don't panic here. Yes, this will definitely make your space look far worse. Like mountains of mess worse. But it's a temporary worse.

If you're cleaning a playroom for example, make little heaps of toy cars, dinosaurs, dolls, etc. If it's the kitchen pantry, put all the crackers, cereal, soup, etc. in their own piles. And then move on to the next step as quickly as possible.

2. Purge, Edit, and Eliminate

After your things are sorted, decide what you want to keep and what you don't.

As you go about decluttering and organizing your home, there are three things you need to ask of all of your things:

IS IT BEAUTIFUL? Of course, we don't just want a clutter-free home. We want one that is lovely too. If you love something because of its beauty—like you'd actually go out and purchase it in the store today—and you have the space for it, it can stay.

Note: beauty is subjective. So what I may find beautiful, you may not. And vice versa. Only you can decide the answer to this question in your house.

IS IT USEFUL? There are a few things that can *just* be beautiful in your home, but there will be many more things that serve a purpose. They are useful items. If you genuinely need something, it can stay.

Now, along with this question there is the additional question, "Is this the only thing that can be useful in its way?" If you have somehow collected three can openers over the years, they're technically all useful . . . but you don't need three can openers! Get rid of two and keep the best one.

IS IT SENTIMENTAL? This one can be a bit of a tricky question to answer. We've likely all been given things from family or friends that we didn't choose to have. But for one reason or another, they hold sentimental value.

For example, my grandmother's china is lovely. It's a classic white bone china with a gold rim. But until recently, I didn't have the space for it, so it lived in a Rubbermaid tote at my sister's until I had room to store it. If you have something similar, you will

need to decide whether to keep it based on space and how much it truly means to you.

Another example from our house: Years ago, I was given my other grandmother's antique deacon's bench. I kept it for a long time. I loved it because I adored her and it belonged to her. But when my style and the size of my house changed, I realized it just wasn't working for us anymore. Now my sister has it.

The sentimental question is something *only* you can answer. But you also have to ask yourself, "Am I keeping something out of guilt? Or a genuine desire to keep it?"

After asking yourself those three questions, trash anything that's broken and unworthy of fixing. Go ahead, toss it. You don't need it. Ask other family members if they want that thing that was passed down from your great-aunt so-and-so before you get rid of it. If they say no, you are free to part with it, guilt-free. Sell anything you think is sellable. Set aside the money you make from this for your decorating fund. (More about that later.) Next, donate to local and national nonprofits any items that are in good shape but that you haven't used in a while or that you've determined you just don't love enough to make the space for. Then sort by season, color, name, or any other way you need to organize what's left in a particular space.

3. Assign Everything a Home

All the items you decided to keep need to have a specific place. Once you have sorted and eliminated, you should have a pretty good idea of how much space you need for each grouping. Assign homes in cupboards, on shelves, or in drawers for these things. Assign places within easy reach to the things you use often. Things that are used infrequently can go up higher or in a slightly less accessible spot.

It's important to note that if you run out of space, you need to go back a step and *purge some more things.* This is life. There is no unending space. We all have a limit and can't keep everything. It doesn't matter whether you live in 500 square feet or 2000 square feet. There is a limit on your space. There will always be more things than space to hold them. It's the nature of our consumer society. You simply can't keep what you don't have space for.

4. Shop for Bins, Baskets, and Containers

This step is my personal favorite—I love shopping! After your "keep items" have a place, you can shop for pretty containers, baskets, labels, or whatever you need to get and stay organized. But be sure to do it after the first three steps have been completed. You don't truly know what you need until you have sorted, eliminated, and assigned homes for your things. It's also a bit of a puzzle to figure out what fits where. Make sure you measure height, width, and depth of shelves and cupboards before buying baskets and bins, though—it's no fun to choose them all only to realize they don't fit the way you thought they would.

Don't forget to shop your own house for containers to corral all the mess and then check places like the dollar store and craft store for some great storage solutions.

5. Label It and Put It All Away

Use a Cricut or Silhouette machine to make pretty labels, buy some on Etsy, or use a label maker for simple labels. You can even use a piece of masking tape and a marker if money is tight (try cutting the tape straight to make it look tidy). Just be sure to label everything so that you (and everyone else in your house) know where to put things away.

6. Maintain, Maintain, Maintain

You need to put things in their place when you are finished with them. If you can't put things back right away, make sure you do it at the end of every day. It shouldn't take more than five minutes in each room to get everything back in its place. You just have to do it.

I'm one of those people who has finally—after years of not—decided it's much better for my personal sanity to come downstairs to a tidy kitchen in the morning. It means that, yes, we're loading dishes into the dishwasher and wiping down counters before bed (because we have kids, I feel like I do this a thousand times a day!) when we're tired. But that means that my morning doesn't feel like it's started "behind the eight ball" in a mess. I also put away the remotes and fluff the pillows on the couch before bed too. It just makes me smile to wake up to an organized and pretty version of our spaces before they get used and messy.

7. Change Systems If Needed

If something in your newly organized system isn't working, change it. There's no need to force yourself to use a system that doesn't work. Tweak the basics that you've started with as you find you need to. The step-by-step stays the same. You just change how or where you put and store things.

For example, we used to keep our spices on a tiered metal rack that Dean made for our last kitchen. I loved it! But after we renovated the kitchen at our current house, there wasn't room for it anymore, so we switched to small Ikea picture ledges on the wall instead. The basics of our spice organization worked. We kept the jars sorted in alphabetical order, but we needed to tweak the other part of it.

So, that's the seven-step method I use throughout our house. If your house is chronically disorganized, or if you feel overwhelmed by all the clutter, just get started. Do the work. Start with a drawer or a cupboard and move on. *There's so much satisfaction that comes with having an organized home! Plus it will make it **so much** easier to function, and it will help you when you're ready to start decorating!*

CHAPTER 5

How to Deal with What's "Hot" and What's "Not"

WHEN YOU'RE READY TO begin decorating your home, it can be very confusing and frustrating to read magazines and websites that are constantly churning out articles about "what's trendy now" and "must-have items" for your home. This is actually one of the things that drives me absolutely batty about the home decor and blogging industry. There's no way you or I can possibly keep up. Let me repeat that: there's NO WAY we can actually keep up with all the home decor trends. But, if you can learn how to embrace *only* the trends you love—*and the ones that work for you and your family*—and forget the rest (because who says you must be trendy anyway?), you can decorate with oh-so-much confidence!

To illustrate what I mean about trends working or not working for your family, let me tell you two little stories about my family.

The first story is all about how I admired all my blogger friends and their pretty white slip-covered couches a few years ago. They were so light and bright and clean. Looking at their rooms was like hearing angels singing. They were stunning. Bloggers I knew and talked to in real life insisted that because they were slipcovers, all that white was easy to keep clean. They swore up and down that it was true. *Just pop them off, throw them in the wash, and they'll be as good as new.*

So, I tried it. Our family bought a white slipcovered Ikea Ektorp sectional.

And it was a nightmare.

Okay, maybe I'm exaggerating. Being a little dramatic even. (*I'm sorry, my sweet blogging friends, I have no idea how you do it!*) But in the month or so that we had white slipcovers on our Ikea Ektorp sofa sectional, my experience was the complete opposite of easy. The edges got dingy. The dog—despite having his paws *thoroughly* wiped every time he came inside— somehow managed to get dirty little puppy paw prints on at least three out of five seat cushions. And the dust and hairs those slipcovers collected?!! Ugh. Not to mention that my kids and hubby were terrified to sit on the couch and get it dirty and thus incur Mommy's wrath. Not exactly the peace-filled, relaxed home atmosphere I had envisioned.

But wait, the story actually gets worse. (Or funnier, depending on how you look at it.)

I decided to wash the slipcovers. Oh my gosh. The sectional is um, large. So it took three loads to fit all the slipcovers into the washer. Fair enough. Our washer wasn't huge. But did you know you're not supposed to dry some Ikea slipcovers? Apparently they might shrink. What on earth?! I didn't have the space or time to wait for the covers to drip dry! So, I put them on air dry in the dryer with no heat. Just to tumble them around a bit. Which worked eventually. Although I'm pretty sure it took about as long as letting them drip dry would have. Oh, and did I mention that I broke the washing machine and

incurred a three-hundred-dollar repair bill for this "oh-so-easy" process?! Even with separating the covers into *three* loads, the washer just couldn't handle it. *Which meant it then decided it should seek revenge— and get lovely black grease marks on every single slipcover as it was breaking!* Which is exactly when I gave up on the white slipcovers and went straight to Ikea—do not pass go, do not collect $200—to buy dark gray ones instead. Which everyone liked better anyway. We've since switched to beige slipcovers. But I don't think I'll ever do white again, no matter how popular it is!

The white slipcover trend definitely did not work for us no matter how much I wanted it to!

The second story is more on the positive side. It's an example of a trend we love and one that works for our family.

We decided to give open shelving a try in our kitchen when it started to pop up as a trend. First, before committing, we dabbled with the idea by removing a couple of cupboard doors in our wee bungalow's kitchen. Let me tell you, it made hosting friends and family in that little kitchen so much easier! Everyone could see where the plates were and grab them easily. All without taking anyone's eye out opening a cupboard door in the process. After that, we installed open shelving in our next two kitchens. The first time was over our coffee bar/mini fridge area for glasses and mugs. The second time, we actually installed two long open shelves for all of our everyday dishes and glassware as the focal point in our kitchen remodel. They work so well for us. Do we have to dust them? Yes. Do all our dishes match? Not exactly. They're all white or plain glass, and collected over time. But they're not matching sets. (More about that later.)

The point is, this trend works for us and the way we live our lives, while the white slipcovered sofa definitely did not.

So, How Do You Deal with What's "In" and What's "Out"?

If I'm completely honest, *I'm not a real big fan of trends.* It's weird, I know. A designer who doesn't follow the latest and greatest trends. Maybe it's because I don't like other people telling me what to do and how to decorate *my* home. Maybe it's because I find it superficial and exhausting to try to guess what the next big thing is. Either way, I believe that trends are rather an annoying beast in the home decor world.

There's no shortage of articles online and off at the start of each year (and the middle of the year and the end of the year) proclaiming what's hot and what's not. People telling you what you should decorate *your* home with. Your personal space. I'd like to know who they think they are? Seriously, I'd like to know who these "experts" are. Yes, yes. They may be designers. But so am I. They make a living making spaces look pretty. So do I. But I'll

never deliberately write something to make you feel bad because you like something I may not.

I don't even follow design trends. When asked, I don't usually know off the top of my head what's trendy in home design and decor. *Not without going and looking it up.* And do you know what? That's okay. We don't have to follow what is popular, hot, "in," or fashionable when it comes to home decor. I think you should decorate with what *you* love. I fully believe that your house is *your house.* My house is my house. I know what I like, so I decorate accordingly. Sometimes that will be "on-trend," sometimes it won't be. But it's my house. It's Dean's house. If we love something that's "over" or passé, who really cares?

I'm all for cheering you on while you embrace whatever style you like for your home. But, there's one thing I'll caution you about: *using something very trendy that you love in a permanent way in your home.*

What I mean by that is, if you love ultra-modern colors like black and red with a geometric pattern, please don't tile a master bathroom in three different kinds of red and black geometric tile . . . and never update anything else in your house to co-ordinate. (I once saw someone do this to a house. The kitchen still had '90s fruit motif tile backsplash, the living room and bedrooms had wall-to-wall carpet, while the master bathroom was all modern with crazy bold tile.)

If you love any kind of trend or style, aside from its limited life span as *the* popular thing, please realize how unlikely it is that *you* will love it forever. And making that kind of bold, permanent statement is going to be hard on your future self and potentially your home's resale value down the road.

Along with this motherly advice, I also beg you not to let "them" make you feel bad. Don't let those articles and designers who predict trends bring you down. Don't let anyone tell you something is not in style anymore and therefore you can't use it. Those articles are written just to get eyeballs on them to increase ad revenue or to sell something. (Selling isn't inherently bad, by the way. But whatever is being sold should help and solve a problem, not cause more confusion.)

If you finally saved up enough to buy that chevron, chalkboard, marquee-lighted mason jar lamp you've had your eye on for months, that's now on some outdated trends list, buy it! **It's *your* money and *your* house!** Do *not* let someone else get you down because you like something they do not.

How to Follow the Trends You *Do* Love

I get a lot of questions about trends and how to decorate on a budget when trends come and go all the time. It's a true concern when you're spending hard-earned money. I get it, really I do. But there are a few trends that I like when they come along. And I'm guessing you do too.

So, what if you happen to like the current trendy look? How do you incorporate it into your house without breaking the bank? Or without losing your ever-loving mind changing things all the time?

From a Christian perspective, it's our duty to steward our possessions well. To be wise and responsible with what God has provided for us. And personally, I believe that we do that best with regard to our decorating and ever-changing trends when we choose to keep the big stuff we buy and decorate with classic and neutral.

That is my simple secret to decorating with trends:

Keep the Big Stuff Classic and Neutral

No wasting money on trends for permanent or long-term investment pieces allowed!

- Don't buy a trendy fabric on a couch that you expect to have for years and years. Buy a simple (perhaps non-white slipcovered?) neutral sofa instead.
- Don't plank your walls if you're not up for removing it when you no longer love it. Just use paint. (And maybe a marker to draw fake shiplap lines if you really want to try the look without commitment.)
- And for the love of Pete, don't tile a bathroom or kitchen in bubblegum-

pink or avocado-green tiles! (Why, just why?) White is classic for tile. You can always dress up the room with bubblegum-pink or avocado towels or accents if those are the colors you love.

Other pieces that should NOT be trendy:

- Large living room furniture
- Dining sets
- Bedroom sets
- Kitchen cabinets

Things that *can* incorporate trends the smart way:

- Throw pillows and blankets
- Candles
- Art
- Accents
- Lighting
- Bedding
- Towels and rugs

Be wise and keep the bigger and more costly items neutral. Then add in the trendy looks you love in the smaller, less-costly and less-permanent items. Keep the peace and money you have and don't fret over imposed trends you supposedly need.

If you keep these loose rules in mind, your future self will thank you. And if you ever sell your house, future buyers will thank you for having the incredible foresight not to burden them with here-today-gone-tomorrow trends!

It is honestly that simple!

CHAPTER 6

75 Budget Decorating Ideas

Now that we've decluttered and gotten a handle on trends, we are almost ready to decorate! But first I want to give you some budget decorating ideas to keep in your back pocket for later. They will help stretch your decorating budget and make your home look lovely too!

The internet is full of cheap decorating ideas. Go ahead, Google "budget decorating ideas." You'll find approximately 166,000,000 results. That's great and all . . . except that I find *lots* of those ideas to be, um, not so pretty. Which is a shame. I don't think decorating on a budget has to be ugly, though. I believe you can be budget savvy and still have a gorgeous home. That you can save your pennies and make your house beautiful at the same time. That expensive and designer things aren't necessary to create lovely spaces.

Of course, no one has an unlimited budget when it comes to decorating (or anything, for that matter!). I've spent the last nine-plus years blogging about ways to get the look for less, no matter what that look is. In the next several pages, you'll find a plethora of budget decorating ideas, a roundup of the best ideas we've found and used in our home.

These are budget decorating ideas that *don't look like* cheap decorating ideas. In fact, after you add them to your home, you'll probably be the only one who knows how inexpensive they really were!

15 Furniture Hacks

Building your own furniture or customizing existing pieces is one of the easiest ways to get the look that you want on a budget. Here are 15 simple and budget-friendly furniture hacks you can try this weekend:

1. Update a skirt-less couch with custom legs. You can find these at Ikea, Etsy, and Home Depot. Choose curvy, straight, metal, or wood depending on your style preference. (More on your personal decorating style coming up!)

2. Can't find the raw wood, French farmhouse look you want for your furniture? Create your own by sanding the dark finish off of cheaper chair legs. Add a little stain or wipe-on wax for dimension and protection afterward.

3. Need a side table but don't have the budget? Create a side table from an upside-down large wire basket, topped with a stained wood circle top. Leave the basket empty, or turn the basket right side up and add a couple of extra throw pillows or blankets for a double-duty storage table!

4. The power of paint is well known in the decorating world. If you have existing wood pieces, you can always give them a coat of paint. Like we did with our secretary desk, or our old pine armoire. Choose any color you like to refinish your piece. There are even paint brands that claim you don't need to sand your furniture first. (Of course, be sure to verify that before you try it!)

5. Ikea LACK tables are very versatile little tables that come in several colors. We have had a few over the years! Spray-paint the legs and sides of one gold or black to dress it up a little. For great adhesion, use spray paint designed for plastic outdoor furniture. You can also add little brass corners to make it look a little like a campaign style table.

6. An oldie but a goodie: If you have old-school wood or metal chairs with upholstered seats, reupholster them using a fresh new fabric and a staple gun. Budget-savvy women have been doing this for decades to breathe new life into their furniture!

7. Create bookcases or shelving from old crates. This one is right out of the first apartment or dorm room handbook. But it can be made to look a little more industrial modern, if you use old crates or make new crates look old with a stencil and some paint. You could add some piano hinges painted black to the corners if you're really into the industrial look!

8. Add custom-fit DIY doors to an Ikea LACK cube shelf. We did this for our son's room, and now he has

an extra clothes cabinet for the low price of an Ikea bookshelf!

9 Create a makeshift sofa table by placing a piece of stained or painted wood on two pretty bar stools. Don't think it will work? We did this at our house—and left it this way for two years before we got around to attaching it to the wall with brackets to replace the stools. No one ever said a thing!

10 Another old standby: Paint a thrifted or hand-me-down dresser and use it as a TV console. So many dressers are the perfect size and shape to hold today's thinner TVs. Plus the drawers can be modified or removed to hold game consoles and other entertainment paraphernalia.

11 Create a simple stained wood headboard by nailing 1" x 6" planks to the wall like we did in two of our master bedrooms. This one is a favorite for budget-conscious decorators!

12 Love the look of farmhouse-style open shelving, but not the price of metal brackets? Paint wooden shelf brackets black to mimic the expensive, black metal farmhouse-style ones and pair with dark walnut-stained boards for less expensive farmhouse-style open shelving.

Convinced you want to build a basic coffee or end table with metal legs, only to panic when you found out the cost of the legs? Use cheap wooden 2" x 2"s painted with metallic paint to mimic metal legs on a DIY table build. We did this with a large square coffee table we built for a contest and then used it for years!

Use Ikea or Michaels rolling carts as handy, storage-filled nightstands. Place a lamp on top and all the bedside necessities below. I've recently seen accessories for these carts like table tops and other add-ons to make them even handier! We have several of these in our house that currently house everything from free weights in the basement to hair products in one of the girls' rooms and art supplies in the other's.

Or use an Ikea or Michaels rolling cart as a bar cart, filled with thrifted, sparkly bar needs. Way less than the cost of a new, traditional style bar cart.

12 Ideas for Walls and Art

Another easy place to save money is on wall treatments and art.

I don't know about you, but I still love a paper calendar. If you have a pretty one, you could frame your favorite pictures from last year's calendar. Hang them in a grid pattern to make a stunning gallery wall. Check thrift stores for these too!

One of my favorite ideas for decorating with family photos is to print them in black and white for a cohesive look. We hang them in a grid pattern on the wall, or prop them together on a picture ledge.

Another popular large scale wall idea for kitchens and dining rooms is to use inexpensive plates in various sizes and shapes hung with plate hangers. You could also display Grandma's china or thrift store plates this way—especially if you only have a few pieces!

Got a piece of art you love, but it's just a wee bit too small for where you want to hang it? Make it look bigger by adding a larger frame "floating" around it. Just nail some 1" x 3"s together and hang on a nail a bit above the existing art.

Use the easy pencil transfer method I mentioned before to make any size art you like.

Simply print out whatever word art or other art you like in large size using the tile function on your printer, scribble on the back with the side of a pencil to create a transfer medium, flip over, and trace the outline onto your canvas or wood. Then fill in with paint.

Create DIY canvas art using the method above, or use any other style art you like and then frame with simple square DIY wood frames stained with your favorite stain.

Print downloadable art or photos as black-and-white engineer prints to get large scale art for way less than traditional printing.

This one has been going for a long time: Frame old book pages or sheet music as art. Bonus points if the pages or music have personal significance to you and your family! I did this in our little white house with sheet music my mother-in-law gave me.

Free printable art can be found just about everywhere you look online, including on my website. For practically free art, print your favorite free prints and frame them. Better yet, make a whole gallery wall from them.

25 Make any scale string art using wood, nails, and string. You can hammer nails into wood in any simple shape and then wind the string or yarn between the nails. Simple shapes like hearts, arrows, and stars work well. Plus, you can customize the colors just by changing the stain you use on the wood and the color of the yarn you choose!

26 Love the look of fancy wallpaper, but not the cost . . . or the work involved? Stencil or draw on the walls instead of buying expensive wallpaper. We stenciled a subtle French script onto our little bungalow's dining room wall and a contrasting gray and white trellis pattern on our backsplit's master bedroom wall.

27 Create curtain rods from either plastic or metal plumbing pipe. Paint the pipe whatever color goes with your decor. It doesn't have to be rustic-looking if you use shiny or colorful paint! Our little white house had an addition that was practically all windows. We painted metal rods black and then only had to buy brackets to hang the curtains. The cost would have been astronomical had we bought regular curtain rods for all those windows. Instead it was one of the least expensive window coverings we ever installed.

8 Kitchen Ideas

Kitchens are an area where you can easily spend big bucks to upgrade. But you can also make some changes with a tight budget that still have a major impact.

Buy new knobs and handles for the kitchen cabinets. Check your local hardware store or online places like Amazon for great deals. Just be sure to measure hole distance for pulls so you get handles that fit your cabinetry's existing holes!

If you can't quite spring for new knobs and pulls yet, you could spray-paint your existing kitchen drawer hardware to give them an update in the meantime.

Cover up worn drawer bottoms and cupboard shelves with pretty and fresh contact paper. My mother used to do this, and it still works like a charm. Plus you can get contact paper pretty cheap at the dollar store.

Paint kitchen cabinets instead of replacing them. Give them a good cleaning and a light sanding. We've done this, and if you use quality paint and a good process, the results are stunning! Just be sure you wash all the degreaser/deglosser off before you paint. (Ask me how I know this!)

Or you could also look at just re-placing the cabinet doors instead of the entire cabinet. Many kitchen cabinets are made in standard sizes, and doors can be bought indi-vidually to fit. Ikea cabinets are not standard and don't fit other boxes, unless you . . .

Make non-standard-sized Ikea cab-inet doors work as replacements on standard kitchen cabinets with trim to update a kitchen. This is how we updated our current kitchen. We painted the trim in a color that matched the new doors so it all blends in well.

Make a DIY spice rack with Ikea picture ledges and canning jars, like we have in our kitchen.

Toe kick from the hardware store or big box store is ridiculously expensive. Use MDF (medium-density fiberboard) cut to size, with good paint, instead of traditional toe kick to save a hundred dollars or more during a kitchen remodel.

8 Ideas for Bathrooms

Believe it or not, you can add a lot of pretty to even the ugliest bathroom with a little imagination and a small budget!

Add teak deck panels to the floor of a cheap shower for a spa look and feel that's water-friendly. Ikea sells some great ones at great prices.

To make your shower and bath look more luxurious, hang two

shower curtains and tie them back like window curtains to frame your tub and shower.

Use extra-long regular window curtains paired with a vinyl liner to hide an ugly tub, like we did with the avocado green tub we had at our backsplit. Hang a rod up high for the curtains and another rod lower for the vinyl liner. Keep the liner tucked into the tub for water repulsion and the curtains outside for camouflage.

Store and display unwrapped inexpensive bars of soap in a large jar for necessities that double as bathroom decor.

Add a dollar store shower pouf and wood brushes in an enamel style

soaps bowl on a shelf or the side of the tub for a little vintage beauty.

Make a bathtub tray from scrap pieces of wood and cabinet handles. Keep in mind, the key for a balanced tray is straight wood with no visible hooks or twists.

Upgrade a standard, cheap-looking, frameless bathroom mirror with a DIY wood frame attached with 3M command strips, as one of our blog contributors did.

Paint your bathroom vanity (with quality paint) and change the knobs. Then add some pretty wood furniture feet or cut-to-size wood spindles to the bottom front (the part that overhangs) to make the vanity look like a custom furniture piece.

9 Paint and Trim Tricks

Oh, paint and trim, how I love thee! There are so many ways to add interest and personality to your home with simple paint and trim. Trim has a way of making a space look finished too.

44 If you can't afford fancy moldings and wainscoting, make a chair rail with inexpensive molding and paint above and below with slightly different shades of the same color or coordinating different colors.

45 If you have plain slab/hollow-core interior doors, add some character by affixing molding to make it look like a newer door.

46 Add some personality by painting the inside of your front door a cheery or dramatic color. We've painted ours aqua, black, and mushroom at different houses.

47 Paint your interior doors black or dark navy to add drama and elegance to your space. Or try a light mushroom taupe that's only slightly darker than your wall color for a subtle color boost.

48 Paint the mantel of a gas fireplace to update it, like we did with ours that was previously stuck in the '90s! You can also paint the brassy vent covers on gas fireplaces by removing them and spraying them with black stove paint so they blend in better.

Shiplap is a popular look in the last few years. If you can't find the real thing and don't want to pay the cost to get expensive moldings, you can always shiplap with plywood. We did that in our kitchen and in our living room. We had the plywood ripped at the hardware store to make the job easier. Then Dean just nailed the strips to the wall. You could glue them too. But we wanted to be able to remove them easily if we wanted to change the look later.

Add coffered ceilings, but use layered doorstop instead of crown molding like we did in our dining room. We saved a ton of money and the look is still on point.

Fake taller baseboards by adding small trim a few inches above existing baseboards. Then paint the baseboards, new trim, and space between them all white (or whatever your trim color is).

Spray-paint anything that you love the shape of but not the color—candlesticks, vases, even plastic toy animals! This works really well on thrifted or dollar-store finds.

6 Tips for Trays and Vignettes

There is something magical about corralling pretty things onto a tray or placing them into a cohesive vignette. Doing so takes the clutter out of a collection of things and makes them look instantly curated and purposeful.

53 Repurpose a framed mirror into a tray by adding felt pads to the back to prevent scratches to surfaces.

54 Add some ambiance by filling glass jars, vases, or jugs with battery-powered fairy or Christmas lights and placing them by a fireplace or on tabletops. This is a great way to add coziness in winter after the holidays are over.

55 Create cake stands (for decor) with raw wood candle holders and wood rounds from the craft store. Add wood beads on a wire wrapped around the stand base to embellish, like our large cake stand. Stain or paint them whatever color you like.

56 Group cheap and thrifted taper candle holders onto a tray for a pretty coffee or side table center-piece. I love to do this for the holidays especially.

57 Make a tray with a discarded cup-board door and some cabinet handles. Add chalkboard paint for fun handwritten messages!

58 Use small bowls to sort and store jewelry on your dresser or to collect discarded jewelry on your desk at

the end of the day. I love Rae Dunn pieces for this. But I've also DIY'd my own with a plain bowl and a sharpie too!

10 Fabric Hacks

Often it's the fabric and soft pieces in a room that can cost the most. But with just a few tricks up your sleeve, you can have beautiful rugs, pillows, and curtains without breaking the bank!

Use long painter's drop cloths for curtains, hung with curtain rings. The reason this is such a popular option is that it works and looks great! To soften your drop cloth curtains, wash them before hemming and hanging them.

Use cheap Ikea sheers folded over and clipped with ring clips to create "ruffled" curtains, like we did on our current house's main floor windows. You could do this with drop cloth curtains too.

Use new pretty tea towels, thrifted sweaters, or small rugs to make less costly throw pillows. I have an envelope throw pillow tutorial on the blog that makes this really easy. Just go to HomeMadeLovely.com and type "DIY easy envelope pillows" into the search bar. Or you can use

iron-on hem tape to make it a no-sew project.

Make a laundry room sink skirt from a drop cloth to disguise a standard cheap laundry tub. Attach with press-on, heavy-duty Velcro.

Sew two or more cheaper small rugs together to make a large rug. Or use iron-on hem fuse tape to attach them!

Make a duvet cover by sewing two flat sheets together on three sides and adding buttons or ties to the fourth side. Use two different sheets to make it reversible. You can always find sheets on sale at big box stores like Homesense or HomeGoods.

Fake the look of hard-to-find or expensive grain sack with fabric paint and painter's tape.

Make a large double-sided table runner from drop cloths and hand-letter it with faux calligraphy. I made one years ago that we still use seasonally now.

Hang curtains high and wide to make windows appear larger. This is the go-to rule for curtains anyway. But it makes a really big difference without any extra money spent.

Stencil fabric—for pillows, curtains, placemats or whatever—with a sharpie. Hand draw words or shapes or use an actual stencil with your marker or fabric paint.

7 Lighting Tricks

Lighting is often overlooked when it comes to decorating. And it's certainly forgotten when one is decorating on a budget. But it shouldn't be. Lighting can set the mood and brighten even the gloomiest rooms. We'll talk more about lighting later too, in chapter 9. In the meantime, here are six lighting tricks that won't cost much at all.

Use plug-in pendant lights for extra lighting that looks luxe. Hang with a simple hook in the ceiling.

Make inexpensive plug-in hanging lights look more substantial by grouping a few together, like we did in our family room.

Add a wall sconce anywhere, even where there's no electrical box! Simply use double-sided tape to adhere a battery-powered puck light to the inside of the shade instead of a traditional lightbulb. Voilà! Instant sconce!

Hide cords along the floor with a hollow plastic shower curtain rod that matches your trim color.

Change lamp shades on table lamps to a modern or current shape rather than buying new lamps. Most big box stores have replacement shades available. Pay attention to how your shades attach to your lamps and buy ones with the same type of attachment.

Swag hanging lights that are not centered to make them look better without hiring an electrician. To do this, install a light with extra chain. Add a ceiling hook in the desired spot and loop your chain over it to swag your lamp to the right spot.

Change your lightbulbs to energy efficient and brighter LED versions as your old bulbs burn out. You'll save lots of money over time with their energy efficiency, but won't break the bank doing the whole house all at once. Pay attention to the warmth of the LED bulbs and try to go with all the same color. For example, all warm white or all cool white, depending on your preference. And if you have dimmer switches or plan to install them, make sure you buy dimmable LED bulbs.

Now that you have loads of ideas for budget decor to refer back to when you begin decorating each room in chapter 9, let's take a look at exactly where to start decorating and how to pull it all together!

PART 3

THE 3-STEP DECORATING PROCESS

CHAPTER 7

Step 1

Find Your Decorating Style

I THINK THAT MANY INTERIOR designers would like you to believe that decorating your home is too hard or even impossible if you don't have a design education, or those elusive "designer genes" that some people supposedly have. But I think that is utter nonsense! God made you in His image, and He is the great Creator! You can definitely learn to decorate your own home.

I couldn't always decorate the way I do now. My first several attempts were horrible failures! But over the last twenty years (and especially in the last ten), I have practiced and practiced and practiced decorating our various homes, as well as a few client homes when I've had time to do so. I have literally spent hours studying photos of homes that I love. I have visited many, many model homes, scoured design and decorating magazines, and pored over high-end catalogs.

With all that practice (and a little design education later on) I finally—*finally*—figured out how to put everything together to make our entire home cozy and beautiful. And now I'm going to save you time and money by walking you through the process I use to do it!

In order to decorate your home with ease, you need to sort out two things:

1. What decorating style you're going to make your own that goes hand-in-hand with the feeling you want to create in your home.

2. What colors you're going to use throughout your home to get that cohesive flow we all want.

These two things are what this chapter and the next are all about and they depend on a few factors:

- If your house has its own dominant style. (*IF it does. Not all do.*)
- What style and colors you love.
- What style and colors your spouse loves. (*If they're the sort that likes design and wants to have a say—some do, some don't.*)
- Which colors are unchangeable and which are changeable in your home.

This section of the book is meant for you to really dig into. Take the time to go through it with a pen and paper or whatever you like to use to take notes, and use the worksheets at the end of the chapter to help you.

We're going to start with identifying your unique decorating style in this chapter. To do this I'm going to ask you a series of questions.

If you're lucky, or you've been working on this for a while already, you may have had a good idea of what your style was before you even picked up this book. If that's you, feel free to skim this section. If you choose to do that, I would suggest that you jot down the gist of your personal decorating style to refer back to later as we put together your whole home decorating plan in the next section.

On the other hand, if you are starting where I did years ago and you don't know what style you like, not to worry. We'll figure it out right now, together.

Your Home's Style

Question 1—Does your home have a dominant architectural style?

The very first style thing we need to consider is your house itself.

Does it have a *dominant* style of its own already?

Many homes do not. For example, most subdivisions built in the last several decades really don't have a distinct architectural style. Your home may be one of these. If so, you won't need to worry about an *architectural* style when planning your *decorating* style.

If your home does have a very dominant architectural style of its own, you *will* need to work with that, at least to some extent. Just how much you have to incorporate that style will depend on how bold and obvious the style is.

On the next few pages, you will see the eight most common dominant house styles that I see regularly in some form or another. Take a moment to look at them.

LOG HOME

Originating as one-room cabins in the woods, log homes have a very distinct rustic look and feel.

CAPE COD

Built with steep roofs and large chimneys, Cape Cods often feature windows flanking the front door as well as upper dormers.

CRAFTSMAN

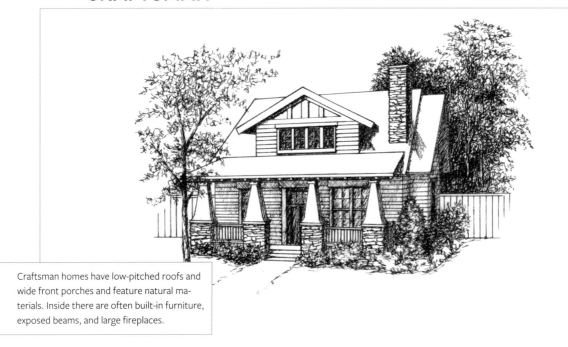

Craftsman homes have low-pitched roofs and wide front porches and feature natural materials. Inside there are often built-in furniture, exposed beams, and large fireplaces.

COLONIAL

Typically a box shape, colonial homes are known for their symmetry, shutters, dormers, columns, and chimneys.

MID-CENTURY MODERN

Mid-century modern homes are usually focused on flat planes, large windows, and seamlessly integrating nature into the home.

MEDITERRANEAN OR SPANISH

Tiled roofs, porticos, arched doorways, and plaster surfaces define Mediterranean or Spanish homes.

TUDOR

Tudors are easily recognizable by their steeply pitched roofs, multiple gables, and decorative half-timber framing.

VICTORIAN

Victorians are typically decorated with ornate trim, bright colors, large porches, and turrets.

After looking at the eight home styles on the previous pages, can you see your house in any of them? Can you pinpoint your home's style easily without much thought? Is it a craftsman or a colonial? mid-century modern or Mediterranean? Tudor or Victorian? Does it have a big wrap-around porch? Or dormers?

If you cannot easily identify your home's style by looking at the *outside* of your house, perhaps the *interior* features will give it away . . .

Does it have a fireplace? Pre-existing built-ins? What do they look like? Are they ornate or plain? Does your house have small windows or large? Are they straight rectangles or are they arched? Are there any other architectural elements that may tell you what style the house is?

If your house has a style that is really strong, you will definitely need to work with that when decorating. For example, you cannot really make a house with Spanish tiles and arched doors look like a log cabin. At least not very well.

Again, if your house has a style that is much less commanding, like say a Cape Cod or a typical suburban, built-in-1999 townhouse that's rather nondescript, *you can pretty much go any direction your heart desires with your decorating style.* You don't have to use your home's architectural style when decorating if it's a very subtle style. And of course if you are in a rental, you can somewhat disregard the style of it and go with what you like. (Although, again, it

may be a hard sell making a Spanish style apartment look like a farmhouse.)

Take a moment to write down what your home's dominant style is, *if any.* Keep this handy as we go through the rest of the chapter.

Your Personal Style

Now that you know what, if any, architectural style you need to work with because of your actual house, let's begin to work out what your unique personal decorating style is. A lot of decorating struggles can be resolved by identifying this. But most people don't accurately know their style, much less are they able to articulate it in any useful manner.

I most certainly didn't know my style when my husband, Dean, and I bought our first house many years ago. We bought all the wrong things—and I don't think we own one single decor item from that house now, all these years later. It makes me sad to think of all the time and money we wasted on decor that didn't last. I want to help you avoid those early mistakes of mine and find your personal decorating style now . . . so you can get on with enjoying your beautifully decorated home already!

Just a note: While you do need to have a handle on your unique style, it can be really tempting to try to pigeonhole yourself into one predetermined style. You may think it's helpful to label your style as fully modern or shabby chic or transitional. But chances are you like elements of more than one style. Keep this in mind while you read the rest of the chapter.

Question 2—How do you want your home to feel?

Let's try a little exercise together.

Close your eyes and visualize your house. Block out everything that's currently *in* your home. Temporarily ignore all the decorating advice you've ever heard before. Yes, even any you may have heard from me! Forget the worn area rug in the living room and the hand-me-down table in the dining room. Turn a blind eye to the sticky fingerprints on the fridge and the paint color on the wall that you hate. Ignore all those things, for just a few minutes.

Now, with your eyes still closed, think about *how you want your home to feel*. What memories of home invoke warm fuzzies for you? How did your home feel when you were growing up? How about your grandparents' house? If you didn't have the greatest childhood at home, in what way would you like your home to be different? How would you like to feel when you walk through your front door? How would you like your family to feel? How would you like your home to feel to your spouse? Your teenager? Your toddler?

Maybe you want a whimsical and fun home. Or maybe a serene and quiet home. Or a combination of those things. There is no wrong answer here. *It's your house!*

How do you want each space to feel? How do you want your home to feel as a whole? Can you imagine it?

Okay, now take a look at the list of words below. Ponder each one. Which ones resonate the most with you? Which ones best describe you and your family?

- Happy
- Relaxed
- Energetic
- Whimsical
- Serene
- Playful
- Comfortable
- Fun
- Warm
- Quirky
- Romantic
- Elegant
- Lighthearted
- Idyllic
- Dignified
- Friendly
- Nostalgic
- Harmonious
- Creative
- Formal
- Peaceful
- Wild
- Open

Consider the individual personalities of your family members. Do you have creatives who would thrive in a vibrant environment? Or would they do better with more limited visual stimulation so they can let their imaginations wander? Do you have quiet thinkers who need cozy corners to curl up in to ponder life? Do you have somewhat wild children who need big open spaces to climb and play? What scents and smells do you remember most about your childhood home? How can you incorporate those into your grown-up home? What does that all *feel* like to you?

Grab a piece of paper, or use the worksheet at the end of the chapter, and make a list of the words you like best and most identify with for yourself and your family members. Maybe even ask your family which ones they like best. Add descriptive words and memories or descriptions of your favorite scents too. Boil this all down to *a few key words* that describe your vision for your family's ideal home environment. If you don't use the worksheet, keep this summary handy as a digital note on your phone or a printed note in your wallet or on your fridge as we go through the rest of this book. It will become an important part of the planning and decorating process.

In my home I have created calm, peaceful spaces with a relaxed and comfortable vibe. There are very few colors in the main rooms, but lots of textures that make our main floor feel cozy. Personally, I find color in those main rooms to be distracting and almost jarring. But in other spaces there's more drama and color. Our kids have all chosen a little more color for their own rooms over the years—navy, black, fuchsia, aqua, blush. Our current basement family room is painted in a dark and moody gray with pops of red, aqua, and yellow that suit the laid-back hangout space well.

Now that you have the feeling you want in your home outlined, we can look into what styles will help you create that feeling.

Question 3—What decor styles are you drawn to?

As you begin defining your personal decorating style, look at the top fourteen decor styles on the next several pages. There are literally dozens of decorating styles, but these are a few of the more popular and easy to identify styles.

BOHO/SCANDI

Boho style decor embraces a carefree, relaxed, and unusual aesthetic. Boho homes are full of life, culture, and the world at large. No two boho homes are alike, much like no two eclectic homes are alike. Originally, boho color schemes emphasized an earthy palette, with deep browns, grays, and greens for base colors and fiery or saturated colors like orange and purple as accents. Today, however, much of boho decor is influenced by Scandi neutral and white colors. Boho is the opposite of minimalist and sleek, opting instead for layers and layers of texture, pattern, and color. Boho/Scandi furniture and decor accessories tend to be found in vintage and thrift stores. However, more and more it can be bought new too for those who like the look but can't necessarily find what they want second-hand.

KEY ELEMENTS OF BOHO/SCANDI STYLE DECOR

- lots of layers and texture
- thrifted and vintage pieces mixed in
- lots of mood lighting, including candles, floor lamps, and table lamps
- opposite of minimalist

- macrame
- plants like snake plants or fiddle leaf fig trees
- either tone-on-tone whites and neutrals or plenty of earthy colors mixed with jewel tones

COASTAL COTTAGE

Cottage is somewhat like the styles of vintage, shabby chic, and retro. But it is very casual and charming. Furniture is often adapted for other uses—like a bench becoming a coffee table. It also tends to be beachy, accented with sea shells and sand-filled jars. Cottage style is airy and light and laid-back.

KEY ELEMENTS OF COTTAGE STYLE DECOR

- ▸ very casual and charming
- ▸ furniture is repurposed
- ▸ beachy and coastal elements, depending on location

- ▸ airy and light
- ▸ monochromatic or shades of blue and green

COUNTRY

Picture pine or painted antiques, quilts, baskets, and folk art. Country decorating can be either simple Americana (often red, white, and blue) or more decorative French country. Colors used in country decorating typically include barn red, mustard yellow, black, dark green, buttermilk, or rust. Ladderback or Windsor chairs, pie safes, tinware, and plaids and checks further depict country decorating. This style is also sometimes called primitive.

KEY ELEMENTS OF COUNTRY STYLE DECOR

- ▸ pine or painted furniture
- ▸ folk art
- ▸ Americana or French country elements

- ▸ barn red, mustard yellow, black, dark green, buttermilk, or rust
- ▸ pie safes, tinware
- ▸ plaids and checks

ECLECTIC

Also known as authentic and original, eclectic decorating throws out all the rules and lets you create something that is uniquely you. Pieces can be drawn from two or three of the other decorating styles. But beware of messy overload! Scale matters and so does color. Think of balancing yin and yang. It's best to keep the basic color palette neutral and then mix and match furniture and accessories as your heart desires. Pair an antique farm table with modern metal chairs. Stack favorite books on a side table. Place a geometric patterned pillow in a bold color on a classic wing chair. Use your imagination.

KEY ELEMENTS OF ECLECTIC STYLE DECOR

- ▸ authentic and original
- ▸ no rules
- ▸ draws from many styles
- ▸ difficult to balance
- ▸ opposites

FARMHOUSE

Shiplap anyone? If you love farmhouse style, you love vintage pieces like old grocery store signs, feed sacks, wide plank floors, barn beams, and plenty of charm. Farmhouse style is full of cozy textures and a balance of old and new that keeps it from looking too theme-y. It's clean and warm, with natural elements brought in from outdoors. It's practical, and not at all fussy or delicate. Matchy-matchy furniture is always a no-no, but especially so with farmhouse style. Farmhouse style, even more than other styles, should look collected over time. There's no rushing a good thing!

KEY ELEMENTS OF FARMHOUSE STYLE DECOR

- wide plank floors
- architectural salvage
- vintage pieces
- reclaimed wood
- barn doors
- apron front sinks
- slipcovers
- rattan/wicker

FRENCH COUNTRY

French country style decor has a casual elegance to it. It's warm and comfortable. The furnishings should have graceful and simple lines, with some curves too. French country style decor features plenty of painted furniture. Buying older furniture and refinishing it with a distressed look would be a perfect fit for this style. Wrought iron or rusted metal accents are sometimes incorporated into this style as well. Fabrics in this style often rely on toile, a very traditional fabric. But the good news is, you can partner toile with stripes, plaids, or solids for plenty of visual interest. French country color schemes can come from all sides of the color wheel. Often this style is paired with the farmhouse look.

KEY ELEMENTS OF FRENCH COUNTRY STYLE DECOR

▸ plaster walls and hefty beams

▸ delicately carved raw wood details

▸ rustic stone floors

▸ old, dark, colorful art on the walls

▸ pottery or baskets for storage

▸ toile!

GLAM

Glam decor is all about luxe and bling. If you love glam, you would happily put chandeliers in every room—yes, every room! Velvet, damask, and even animal prints fit into this look. Glam art may look serious at first glance, but it has a bit of sassiness to it. Delicate details and a flair for the dramatic are also hallmarks of glam style decor. Gold and other shiny finishes are often paired with pink or jewel tones. Another hint that you may like glam decor? All your favorite movies are in black and white!

KEY ELEMENTS OF GLAM STYLE DECOR

- velvet
- chandeliers
- sassy art
- gold or other shiny metals
- pink or jewel tones

INDUSTRIAL

Industrial style takes its cues from old factories and industrial spaces. Exposed brick, stone, and ductwork are all markers of the style. Industrial design incorporates raw, unfinished surfaces, neutral tones, utilitarian objects, and wood and metal surfaces. Industrial style is somewhat minimalistic and often features polished concrete floors. Wood floors are also an option in industrial decor.

KEY ELEMENTS OF INDUSTRIAL STYLE DECOR

- ▸ exposed brick and ductwork
- ▸ stainless steel counters
- ▸ metal walls and doors

- ▸ vintage furniture and accessories
- ▸ open concept spaces
- ▸ industrial lighting in residential settings

MID-CENTURY MODERN

Mid-century modern decor is classic *Mad Men* style at its finest. It's a term that broadly describes decor from roughly the mid-1930s to the mid-1960s. Mid-century modern style consists of a classic understated look with clean, no-fuss lines. The key is not to replicate the look of the era exactly, but rather to incorporate pieces from the period into today's decor. Generally one large piece will set the tone nicely. Don't get too matchy-matchy!

KEY ELEMENTS OF MID-CENTURY MODERN STYLE DECOR

- ▸ functionality before style
- ▸ uncluttered lines
- ▸ organic shapes
- ▸ juxtaposition (like hairpin legs on a large dresser)
- ▸ multiple finishes like plastic, wood, and metal

MINIMAL

Minimalism means spacious rooms with minimal decor and accessories. Minimal decor is achieved through the use of functional furniture and geometric shapes and limiting colors to one or two. Open-concept homes are especially useful in minimal decor.

KEY ELEMENTS OF MINIMAL STYLE DECOR

- simplicity
- straight lines
- lots of light
- open spaces
- absence of patterns
- less is more

RUSTIC

Rustic design is comprised of rugged, natural beauty with simple and earthy colors. It tends to be heavier, darker, and more masculine than other decor styles. Rustic decor is also comforting and fuss-free. Materials in rustic design are often wood and natural stone. Aside from logs in a log cabin, shapes are generally organic and abstract.

KEY ELEMENTS OF RUSTIC STYLE DECOR

- ▸ warm tones
- ▸ wood and stone
- ▸ neutral colors
- ▸ heavy and masculine

SHABBY CHIC

Made popular by Rachel Ashwell and her retail chain in the 1980s, shabby chic decorating combines the idea that something worn and perhaps dilapidated can also be elegant and stylish. Simple slipcovers, flower arrangements like roses or hydrangeas, chippy painted or whitewashed wood furniture and shades of white (and other soft colors) are indicative of shabby chic decorating. So are vintage mirrors, spray-painted formerly brass chandeliers with hanging crystals, and handcrafted and vintage items as opposed to mass-produced.

KEY ELEMENTS OF SHABBY CHIC STYLE DECOR

- worn and timeless
- elegant and stylish
- slipcovers, flowers
- chippy paint and whitewash
- not mass-produced

TRADITIONAL

Traditional decorating is calm, orderly, predictable, and full of classic lines and understated details. Furniture is often in matching sets—like a complete dining room set or perfectly matching coffee table and end tables. Think wall sconces, tassel-trimmed full drapery, wing chairs, extensive moldings, highly polished dark cherry or mahogany wood. Fabrics include silk, velvet, and damask. Accessories tend toward ornate gilded mirrors and artwork inspired by nature. Furniture layouts are quite formal and placed at right angles from each other. You like to keep it even and organized, tried and true with traditional decorating.

KEY ELEMENTS OF TRADITIONAL STYLE DECOR

- ▸ typical of older generations
- ▸ calm, orderly, predictable
- ▸ classic lines and understated details
- ▸ full drapery, wing chairs, matching sets
- ▸ silk, velvet, damask
- ▸ extensive moldings
- ▸ right angles

TRANSITIONAL

Transitional design is somewhat difficult to pin down but by definition is a combination of two opposite styles. In practice, it's a mix of traditional design with modern elements. Think traditional wainscoting and antiques paired with clean-lined modern pieces. But it's not a hodgepodge like eclectic decor is. It's more like a younger version of traditional design. It's timeless with a hint of the current.

KEY ELEMENTS OF TRANSITIONAL STYLE DECOR

- neutral colors or neutrals with subtle hints of one or two colors
- mixed textures

- limited accessories
- impactful art
- comfortable furniture

Which of the decorating styles did you most identify with? Which one is your most favorite? Your second favorite? Which one best describes your home? Or maybe I should ask, Which one describes the home you'd like to create? Write this down on the worksheet or near where you wrote down how you want your home to feel. If you think you like a few styles, jot down specifically the elements from each that you like. *I have a style quiz on my website that can help you figure this out. Just go to HomeMadeLovely.com and search for "style quiz."*

While we walk through the next few questions, and while you're looking at photos and inspiration you may have collected, I want to point out that you now need to focus on the *individual elements* in the inspiration images. Yes, the overall feeling in each one is helpful, obviously. But after noticing how a space makes you feel, you need to pay special attention to the details. Things like the:

- Shape of the furniture—Is it round and curvy? Does it have straight lines? Is there button tufting? What wood finish does it have?
- Accessories—Do you like shiny accents? Or chippy wood pieces? Or ones with vibrant pops of color?
- Layout—Does the floor plan seem open and airy? Or is it more traditional, with clearly separated rooms?
- Color scheme—Is there lots of color? Or are your inspiration im-

ages full of more muted, neutral colors?

Let's look at a few places that may hold clues to your style.

Question 4—What do your Pinterest boards tell you?

Pinterest can be a fabulous tool in your decorating tool belt. But most of us just scroll aimlessly and pin pretty photos while we're lying in bed with insomnia because we had one too many lattes or while we patiently (or not so patiently?) sit in the pickup lane at our kids' school. But most of us never go back to those pins or boards again, which is such a waste of a great resource.

Instead of just pinning and pinning without ever putting those saved pins and boards to use, we're going to use them now to help you uncover your style.

With this book in hand, go to your Pinterest account and click on the page with all your boards. (If you don't have a Pinterest account, set one up today and follow me at Pinterest.com/HomeMadeLovely!) Do you have a board dedicated to home inspiration? Maybe more than one? What are some of your favorite home image pins on those boards? Which ones express the feeling you want to convey in your home?

Now really look at each of those saved photos. Examine the individual elements. The light fixtures, the rugs, the furniture, the lines. The details.

What do the photos tell you about the decorating style you may like? What colors do your favorite images have in common? Are the photos rich in texture? Are they filled with collections or are they clean and minimalistic? What colors are repeated? What textures? Materials?

Bonus Tip: Have a friend look at your Pinterest boards too. Ask her what commonalities she sees in the images you've pinned. What colors, styles, patterns jump out at her?

Use the worksheet or your phone to make a note of the things you (and your friend) notice about the images on your Pinterest boards.

Question 5—What magazines do you love?

Whether you read design magazines in their online format or in their traditional printed medium, have a subscription or just occasionally peruse your favorites at the bookstore, the magazines you read can give you clues to your decorating style.

What are the titles of some of your favorite magazines? Do you read *Cottages and Bungalows*? Or is *Magnolia Journal* more your thing? Does that give you any hints as to your personal decorating style preferences?

Are there any special feature publications you are drawn to again and again each time they're published? Such as an annual white issue or the cottage issue?

What possible themes run through all of the magazines you read?

Write down on the worksheet or in your notes the titles of the magazines that you absolutely adore. Especially the ones you have a subscription to. Take note of their overarching decor themes and small details. If you don't subscribe to any magazines, consider visiting your local bookstore to look through the ones you're drawn to.

Question 6—What home decor blogs do you regularly read?

Do you have any favorite home design or decor blogs? Do you love any blog so much that you subscribe to their email list? (We all know that if you gave them your email address, you *really* love them!) Which ones?

How do the writers of those blogs describe their home decor style? What words do they use? What colors do they always decorate with? Or do they use neutrals with a lot of texture? How do you feel when you look at photos of their homes?

Write these things down too on the worksheet or in your notes.

Question 7—What shows and movies do you binge watch because of their decor?

If you had an hour to watch TV, and you only had HGTV, the DIY Network, or W to watch, which show would you choose?

Which decorators or designers can't you get enough of? What colors do they use? Do they always buy new, have things custom-made, or buy from thrift shops?

Conversely, which designers don't you love? Why? What don't you like about their style?

What movie homes do you love? What do those homes have in common? Ceiling-high bookshelves? Bold blocks of color? Subtle whites and creams?

What HGTV shows or movies do you return to again and again because you adore the houses?

Jot down on the worksheet or in your notes what movies and TV shows you love for the decor and why.

Question 8—What are your favorite home decor shops?

If I gave you $1,000 (I honestly wish I could!) and you had to spend it on decorating, which store would you run to first? What stores have you absolutely drooling over the decor? Where do you go to window shop? What are your favorite big box stores or small local boutiques? Why are they your favorites? What Etsy shops and makers do you love? Why? What do you love about them?

Write this down too.

Putting Your Style Together

Those eight questions should have given you a great deal of insight into your design style.

Look at your notes again and compile a list of the things that are common or repeated from all the questions.

Write down the answers to a few more questions:

- What colors are you always drawn to?

- What wood finishes (light, medium, dark) do you prefer?
- Do you love antiques or newer, modern pieces?
- Do you like straight lines or more ornate shapes? Or a mix?
- What fabrics seem to draw you in? What patterns do you love (feminine florals, geometrics)?
- What words express the feeling you notice in all the spaces you love?

It will likely take about an hour to read through the common decorating styles and to thoughtfully go through the questions looking for hints of your style. If it takes you longer that's okay too. Just make sure you jot down your answers to all the questions before you move on and especially before you purchase one more thing for your house.

Finally, boil your style down to a one- or two-paragraph description. Give it a name if you like.

Remember to stay positive while you're doing this exercise and answering the questions. No whining and complaining or comparing your current home to your inspiration photos. You'll get there in time. As the saying goes, "Don't compare your beginning to someone else's middle."

Once you know your own personal decorating style, you will be able to decorate with confidence, knowing you aren't wasting your time or your money anymore!

How to Decorate as a Couple

If you are going through this whole decorating process and you're married to someone who has a lot to say about decor and design, along with your house's style and your personal decorating style, you may have to contend with your partner's decorating style too.

Perhaps you believe you know your spouse inside out and backward. But in the past, when you've purchased something you absolutely adore for your space, you're completely floored to find out that they really dislike it. (Like when I found out Dean hates cucumbers after twenty years of marriage!)

Don't freak out! This is totally normal. Decorating style is incredibly personal and even your soul mate may like or dislike very different decorating styles than you. And likes and dislikes can change over time too.

Here are a few ways to navigate decorating your home as a couple:

1. Decide on an objective. Is this a drastic makeover or just a little refresh? When you both know what to expect, it's much easier to negotiate the specifics.

2. Decide what stays and what goes. Do you have any pieces that you love? What about your spouse? Negotiate and compromise to sort out what is really important to each of you. Put this in writing if needed to keep you both focused.

3. Decide what items need both partners to sign off on before purchasing. Is it just the big stuff like the couch and the TV, or is it all the small accents as well? Can one of you choose the curtains and rug, or do you both need to have a say? Again, write it down if necessary.

4. If your spouse is very particular about the decor in your home, or seems to always surprise you with what they like and don't like, have them go through the beginning of this chapter on their own too to get a handle on what they like. Then combine both your results to come up with a unique decorating style that suits both of you.

5. Go shopping together. Sometimes just the act of choosing something together can make all the difference. Take your time, especially if you don't know each other's style very well. Try to go out when you are both relaxed and well-rested. We all know how quickly being tired and hungry can turn into being disastrously hangry!

Remember to pick your battles wisely and remain patient with each other. Decorating your home matters. But your marriage matters much, much more!

Now, let's talk about the colors you love and how that plays into your master decorating plan!

FIND YOUR HOME'S ARCHITECTURAL STYLE

1. Look at the eight common architectural styles on the previous pages and then jot down notes about the possible *exterior* style of your home.

2. Does your home have a fireplace? Pre-existing built-ins? Small windows or large? Any other architectural elements that may tell you what style the space already is? Write down the possible interior style your home may be.

3. Based on the answers above, does your home have a very dominant style that you will need to work with? If so, what is it? (Remember if it doesn't, you don't need to worry about this step.)

HOW DO YOU WANT YOUR HOME TO FEEL?

TAKE YOUR EMOTIONAL TEMPERATURE

When you're beginning to decorate your home, you need to take a step back. Take a deep breath. And ignore everything that's currently in your home. Forget all of the *things*—and focus on the *feelings*.

How do you want your home to feel? Check all that apply. But be choosy.

☐ Happy	☐ Comfortable	☐ Lighthearted	☐ Creative
☐ Relaxed	☐ Warm	☐ Idyllic	☐ Formal
☐ Whimsical	☐ Fun	☐ Dignified	☐ Peaceful
☐ Energetic	☐ Quirky	☐ Friendly	☐ Relaxed
☐ Playful	☐ Romantic	☐ Nostalgic	☐ Open
☐ Serene	☐ Elegant	☐ Harmonious	☐ Wild

On the lines below, jot down any other words or feelings you can think of that express how you want your home to feel. Keep this worksheet handy because you'll want to refer back to it when we look further at your preferred decorating styles.

_____

_____

_____

FIND YOUR PERSONAL DECORATING STYLE

1. From the Emotional Temperature worksheet, what were the top three feelings you want to convey in your house?

_____

_____

2. If your home has a dominant style of its own, what is it?

_____

3. Look at the fourteen decorating styles. Which ones do you like? Jot down a few.

_____

_____

_____

4. What style information can you glean from your Pinterest boards and pins? What colors are repeated? What textures? Materials?

_____

_____

_____

5. Write down the titles of the magazines that you absolutely adore. Take note of their overarching themes and small details.

_____

_____

_____

6. What decor blogs do you read? Which ones do you subscribe to? What styles do the authors say that their homes are? Are their homes colorful or full of neutrals?

_____

_____

_____

7. What HGTV shows or movies do you return to again and again, at least in part because you adore the houses?

_____

_____

_____

8. What home decor stores are your hands-down favorites? Which one(s) would you run to if you were given $1,000 to spend on decor? What would you buy?

_____

_____

_____

9. Given the feelings you said you want to convey in your home, your home's dominant style (if applicable), your thoughts on the fourteen decorating styles, and your answers to the other questions on this worksheet, which styles do you like most?

10. Now sort the styles from question 9: Write down your top three preferred styles in order from most liked to least below. These make up your unique style.

11. Give your unique style a description and, if desired, a name.

For more details on how to choose and incorporate your unique style into your home, be sure to check out my decorating course at DecoratingUncomplicated.com.

CHAPTER 8

Step 2

Create Your Master Plan

NOW THAT YOU'VE GOTTEN a good grasp on how you want your home to feel and what style you (and your spouse) prefer, you may be thinking a little more about how to make all the spaces look cohesive and flow well together decoratively.

As I mentioned at the beginning of the last chapter, there are two keys to decorating your home so that you get cohesive flow throughout.

1. Decorating Style

Choosing your own unique decorating style *and committing to it* is the first way to create cohesive flow throughout your house. You definitely need to know what style elements you love. And once you choose your unique and personal decorating style, you need to stick to it. That means no getting distracted by things that don't fit that style. We did the hard work of uncovering your unique style in the last chapter. Don't undo it by being wishy-washy with it now.

2. Color

The color scheme you choose to use in your home is the fastest, cheapest, and least complicated way to create a unified and beautiful look throughout your house. This can even be utilized in a rental or dorm space. And it can be done using items you already have or with new items, and no matter what flooring or trim you have.

In order to learn how to use color to create a unified look, we're going to learn just enough color theory so you have a base of knowledge to work from.

What makes a good color combination? I mean, what makes some colors work really well together and some, well, not so much? The answer is in color theory.

You may have heard of color theory before, perhaps in college or on your favorite design show. But perhaps you never quite got the hang of all these terms and their rules.

I want to reassure you that practical color theory for decorating is actually pretty simple when it's broken down and you learn just enough.

So, let's learn just enough . . .

THE COLOR WHEEL The easiest starting point for learning about color theory is the color wheel. The color wheel has all the colors of the rainbow on it. From it you can choose all sorts of fun color combinations.

The color wheel simply helps us to identify the basic colors of four main types of color schemes.

COLOR THEORY TERMS

- ▸ **Hue:** another word for color
- ▸ **Tint:** adding white to a color
- ▸ **Tone:** adding gray to a color
- ▸ **Shade:** adding black to a color

4 Main Types of Color Schemes

There are four main color schemes that you can use in your decorating. Each one requires choosing a main color and then choosing other colors to go with it.

1. Monochromatic

This color scheme uses *any one color and its various shades, tints, or tones.* This scheme is very easy to implement and is a good place to start if you are unsure of yourself and your color choice, *or* if you like a subdued and subtle look. I use this color scheme a lot in our house, with shades of warm white.

2. Two-Color or Complementary

This color scheme uses *any two colors that are directly opposite each other on the color wheel.* This scheme is typically a high-contrast look with colors such as red and green, orange and blue, or even pink and muted green.

3. Multi-Color or Split-Complementary

This color scheme utilizes *one main color and the two colors on either side of its opposite.* It offers a rather dramatic look. An example of split-complementary color scheme would be red, aqua blue and yellow-green because red is opposite green, and green has aqua blue and yellow-green on either side of it.

4. Related or Analogous

This color scheme uses *one main color and up to six neighbors* next to it on the color wheel. For example, blues and greens which are next to each other on the color wheel.

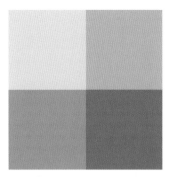

Monochromatic

Two-color or complementary

Multi-color or split-complementary

Related or analogous

Understanding Undertones

After you've decided what sort of color scheme you like, you should know something about undertones of colors.

Even if you love to decorate with neutrals, you are actually decorating with color, because every shade of neutral other than pure white and pure black is a color and has a color undertone.

The undertones in paint and furnishings are necessary to successfully choosing any and all colors of everything for your house. You'll want to figure out whether you have/want:

1. Cool colors—green, blue, or purple undertones; cool colors calm and soothe. They also recede, making spaces seem larger.
2. Warm colors—red, orange, or yellow undertones; warm colors are warm and cozy. They appear to come closer, making spaces seem smaller.

If you don't want to examine your colors too intently, just decide whether a color looks warm or cool to you and what kind of mood you want your space to have. Remember that warm colors tend to create coziness, while cool colors are soothing.

Two Tricks for Finding the Undertone of Something (Works for Paint Colors and Decor)

You cannot see the undertone in a color without comparing it to another color! Do not look at your colors in isolation. If you look at a white by itself, it will just look white. But when you put it next to TRUE white, it may look yellow or pink or even green.

1. One simple trick to finding the undertone of a color is to **hold it up next to a color wheel and see what color it most looks like.**
2. *Or* **place the color you're considering next to a *pure* version of that color. The undertone should reveal itself.** For example, if you're looking at a blue-colored paint chip, hold pure, primary blue next to it for comparison. If you're looking at a white slipcover, hold up a true white next to it to see the fabric's undertones.

The easiest way to find the undertone of a paint color is to look at the bottom of the paint swatch—if the bottom color has green in it, the upper colors will too. If it is a pink color, the upper colors will have pink in them too.

Any of these methods make it much easier to successfully choose colors with the correct undertone (especially whites or neutrals).

Pay Attention to Lighting

How much and what type of lighting in a room will also affect the colors in a space. For example, blue northern light will emphasize blue undertones; golden southern light will make colors appear creamier. Your light fixtures can also affect the way your colors appear. Typical lightbulbs will cast a warm yellow glow, while fluorescent lighting adds more of a green tint. This is why I am going to tell you to test colors IN the actual space before you paint and decorate.

How to Use Undertones

There are a few schools of thought when it comes to undertones.

1. **Use all warm or all cool undertones.** This is the easiest method for beginners to use. However, the results are sometimes a "flat" color scheme, leaving spaces occasionally feeling like there's something missing.
2. **Use a mix of warm and cool undertones.** Some say 80 percent of one and 20 percent of another, while others say an even mix.

However, there really are no hard and fast rules and any percentages are given as guidelines to help beginner decorators!

The Right Way to Choose Paint Colors—and the Two Things You Should Never Do

Lots of people make one huge mistake when decorating. (Well, they make more, but let's stick with just this one for now.) They choose paint colors first. But **paint colors should *never* be the first thing you select for a room.** You should always choose large furniture items or things like a statement rug for your room before choosing your paint colors. You can even **use a large piece of fabric in a pattern and colors you love to draw color inspiration from.**

Really, please hear me . . . **if you do not have the major inspiration piece for a room yet, please do not choose paint colors until you do.** That is the first thing you should never do. A professional designer would NEVER decide on a paint color first!

Okay, so aside from having your big piece(s) first, do you want to know my number two rule for choosing paint colors?

Just to remind you, I have to say I don't actually have very many rules for decorating at all. I think there are very few that *must* be followed. The rest can usually be bent or broken altogether. But there's NO BREAKING this one. If everyone would just follow this one rule for choosing paint colors it would prevent 100 percent of bad paint choices. Okay, so I don't know the actual percentage. But every time I see someone doing this at the paint or hardware store, I feel like I may just lose my mind. It's all I can do to not be a paint Nazi and police the paint aisle on a Saturday afternoon. Because I know it's going to be totally awful and heartbreaking when they do this.

So here it is . . . the second rule you MUST follow: *Do not choose paint colors at the store!*

For the love of Pete, just don't do it!

Paint is made up of different colors with different undertones. You just learned this! The only simple colors are full-on primary colors—red, blue, and yellow. But no one wants those colors outside of a kindergarten classroom!

When you pick a paint color at the store, it's usually under yellow fluorescent lighting, right? Well that yellow lighting changes the way all paint colors look to our eyes because of the undertones. Yes, those undertones.

Paint simply will not look the same at home as it does in the store. EVER!

The right way to pick paint colors:

1. **Choose your main fabric and/ or multi-colored inspiration item FIRST!**
2. After you have your inspiration pieces, **choose a few paint swatches and bring them home with you.** Look at the undertones in your furniture, rugs, etc. and choose paint swatches accordingly. Remember to look at the bottom color on the paint swatch to see its undertone. Tape the swatches to the wall. Or buy sample pots and try a few shades on the wall in the room you want to paint.
3. Once your paint samples are up, place some of the accents—flooring if it's not yet laid, furniture, pillows—in the room to see how they look with the paint swatches or samples.
4. Now **look at the paint paired with your decor in different lighting at different times of day.** Look at them with lights on and lights off. Look at them early in the day, in the afternoon sunlight, and in the evening. Choose what looks best in the space with the accents and actual lighting. Write this color down.

It becomes *so much* easier to choose paint colors well when you see them in their true surroundings.

Creating a Color Scheme for Your Whole Home

So, you've decided how you want your home to feel, you've defined a decorating style, and we've talked about color schemes and undertones. Hopefully, you've taken a look at a decorator's color wheel and looked at some paint chips to see their undertones to get a feel for them. Now you're going to use that knowledge to create a color scheme for your entire home.

If you recall, **cool colors are soothing and warm colors are cozy.** So you will want to choose colors that work with the feeling you want to convey in your home and the unique style you created for your home. You can choose one main undertone and use the opposite in small accents (using the 80–20 rule). If you're really unsure of yourself and colors, start by only using *either* warm or cool colors and save the mixing of them for later.

How to Create a Whole Home Color Scheme

After reading the previous sections about undertones, choosing paint, and lighting, you're going to choose five colors total: *a white, a neutral, and three colors, plus wood and metal tones.* **Here's how to do it:**

1. When you're planning colors for your home, you need to take stock of the unchangeable elements in your home: the things that are essentially permanent, like flooring, kitchen and bathroom cabinets, countertops, faucets, and wall tiles. Unless you're planning on renovating these as you decorate, they are fixed and—like it or not—play into the color schemes you will choose for your decorating. Note the color and undertones (warm or cool) of your fixed elements.

2. Observe the major wood tones in your home. If you have dark walnut hardwood floors throughout your home and you don't plan to change those, that is automatically your major wood tone. Or if you

have oak cabinets in your kitchen, oak railings by your stairs, and oak cabinets in your bathroom, *that* is automatically your major wood tone. You can choose 1–2 secondary wood tones as well to use in occasional furniture pieces like side tables and chairs. But pay attention to the undertones in the existing (or, if you're renovating or building, the planned) wood items.

3. Observe the metal finishes in your home. Metal items also have undertones that play to the colors on the color wheel. Golds and bronzes have yellow-orange undertones and are warm-toned metals, while silver and chrome are ever so slightly blue and are therefore cool-toned metals. Make note of what metal finishes are already in your home and/or what you want to change those to.

4. Consider the piece that is visually the largest in each room: the sofa or rug in your living room, the bedding or rug in your bedroom, the cabinets and counters in your kitchen. What colors or undertones do those have?

5. Choose either a warm or cool white paint color to carry throughout your home. This will be the color of your trim, interior doors,

and ceilings. (You can paint your interior doors in one of your other colors later if you're feeling brave!)

Choose which neutral to use throughout your whole home: white, taupe, beige, or gray. This will be the basic color that can carry through on the walls wherever you want something subdued or when you're not sure what else to use. It's great for hallways and large open-concept spaces, as well as large furniture pieces.

Choose three other colors to use throughout your house, using one of the four color schemes from the color theory lesson (monochromatic, complementary, split-complementary, or analogous). These will be the colors you pull from a fabric you love, or a large area rug, or even a sofa. Remember, these are the general colors of your decor scheme and not paint colors yet. (Those are coming.)

The 60-30-10 Rule—or How to Use Your Colors

Now that you've chosen your five colors (a white, a neutral, and three colors), we're going to break this down into which colors you will use in each room.

Remember, one of the ways to get cohesive flow in your home is by using consistent color throughout. But how do you do that . . . without everything looking the same?

You use the colors you've chosen in different proportions in different rooms!

The 60-30-10 rule is a timeless decorating rule that can help you put together your color scheme with ease. The 60, 30, and 10 percent proportions help you break down your colors and give balance to your space visually. It's also super easy to follow and implement.

- 60 percent will be the main color of your room. This will likely be the general color of your walls, and perhaps your sofa and rug. This 60 percent anchors the space and provides a backdrop for other colors.
- 30 percent will be the secondary color in a room. It's—obviously—half the amount of the main color. This can be used in accent furniture, curtains, and bed linens.
- 10 percent will be the accent color of a room. This would be used in throw pillows, accessories, art, etc.

So how does the 60-30-10 rule work in practice?

Let's say you've chosen a warm white for your trim and doors, a taupe for your neutral, plus a brown, a red, and a blue. You could implement those colors this way:

- 60 percent taupe, 30 percent brown, and 10 percent blue in the living room (taupe walls and rug, brown leather couch, blue throw pillows)

- 60 percent taupe, 30 percent blue, and 10 percent red in the master bedroom (taupe walls and bedspread, blue accent wall, and red throw pillows)
- 60 percent blue, 30 percent taupe, and 10 percent red in the powder room (blue walls for drama, taupe towels and floor tiles, and red accents)

Do you see what I mean? You're using the same colors throughout the house, but you're using different proportions in each individual space.

Remember, not every one of your colors has to be used in every room, nor do the percentages have to be exact! They are just for guidance! Also note that not all the colors are necessarily solid colors. You can implement patterns in these color percentages.

Using the worksheets, decide in which proportions you will use each of your colors for every room in your house. Remember, the colors can be in the form of paint on the walls, furniture, rugs, draperies, accents, and art. Then take it to the final step and choose your paint colors for each room using your large pieces and general colors as a guide. *Keep these worksheets handy! You will need to refer to them when we start decorating!*

Beginning to Plan for Each Room in the House

Once you've gotten the general and paint colors worked out for your whole house, you need to take a closer look at each room individually. Not so that you can plan them all in detail yet, but so that you have a general idea of the direction of each space and so that you can plan out your decorating budget, which you will need to help you decide which room to work on first in the next chapter.

Define each room's purpose

First, with a notebook in hand, walk through *each room* making note of:

- All the activities that take place there
- The repairs that need to occur
- Any items you would like to add to the space
- The furniture you need to make the space function well for you and your family
- Which of those pieces you already have
- Which ones you still need to find

Make sure to do this for every room. Be thorough.

Outline a budget for decorating

In order to know which room to work on when, you need a loose budget for each space. By planning this out in advance, you can make more educated decisions when it's time to actually start on a room. Here's how to create a budget for decorating:

1. ORGANIZE YOUR LIST. After you've walked through each room to make note of what its purpose is and what it needs, walk through each room again. In each one, look at the notes you made about it. Look at the needed and desired items on your list. Rewrite the list in order starting with the most wanted or needed items at the top and go down from there.

2. RESEARCH PRICING. Do some quick on-line research to find pricing for the things on your list. Look at a few websites for options, comparing prices and availability. Do *not* buy anything yet! After gathering this info, allocate a price to each item on the wish list.

After you have individual item pricing, you need to add a little cushion to your budget, especially if you're doing any renovations. Renos notoriously go over budget. So if you plan for that, you won't be caught off guard. Even if you're only buying decor, adding a buffer of 10 percent to the overall budget can really help cushion you, should pricing change or you need more paint, or you didn't buy enough flooring the first go-round.

With this in mind, write down the approximate total for each room. Don't get discouraged. This is a very eye-opening exercise. It helps you to plan well. And it helps to educate you on what you *truly* want for your home.

3. START SAVING. Saving for decorating works just like saving for anything. Set up a bank account that you will use just for decorating. Use online banking at a bank that offers no-fee banking and transfer money to that account as you go to make it easier. If you skip coffee today so you can save up for that throw pillow, transfer the money into the decorating account right away. If you are really serious about saving to make home your happy place, temporarily reduce your cable package, negotiate new rates on your insurance and phone bills, eat out a little less, or switch banks to one that has lower or no fees. Put money aside little by little.

Another way to gain money for decorating is to declutter, purge, and sell anything that you will not be using in your new decor. You could have a decor sale if you have decor that you simply outgrew, but that someone else may love. Try a garage sale. Maybe sell items on eBay or Kijiji/Craigslist. It may not be possible to fund your new decor plans entirely with this method, but you could get quite a jump start on them!

4. ADJUST IF NEEDED. Make adjustments to your wish list based on *when you want to finish decorating and how much you can have saved in that time*. The reason we put the items in order of want/need is that **no one** can afford everything on their wish lists. We all need to make adjustments to our lists. And we may have to compromise and wait awhile for the things that aren't as important.

It can be really easy to spend a lot of money on decorating. But it's much easier to rein it in when you actually have a plan in place. Plus your house will thank you for not filling it with spur-of-the moment purchases that just don't work well together and end up as clutter!

I know coming up with this master plan for your home may seem counterintuitive to what the world says about the creative process—that it should be full of free-spirited expression with no limits or imposed rules. But our Creator God is a planner. He created the earth in a specific order, on specific days. There was still creating and creativity. But it was organized. There was a framework and a structure to it.

That is exactly what we've created in this chapter. A framework for you to follow. A plan that lays out everything in detail.

With that done, we can move onto the next chapter, working on one room at a time in the right order, so that you can create the home you've always envisioned for yourself and your family.

CREATING A WHOLE HOME COLOR SCHEME

Using the information you learned about color theory, and a color wheel, fill out these worksheets to find a cohesive color scheme for your house.

1. What colors are fixed and can't be changed?

a. Write down all the current unchangeable items in your home such as the flooring, countertops, and wood trim that won't be painted. Observe the wood tones and metal finishes. Next to each item write down its color undertone.

UNCHANGEABLE ELEMENT	UNDERTONE

b. What is the existing dominate undertone in your home? (Circle one.)

COOL (cool white, beige, brown, greens, blues and violets)

WARM (warm white, gray, black, reds, oranges and yellows)?

2. Which season of colors do you like best in your home? (Circle or highlight one.)

SPRING: light, bright and airy, pastels like pink and green

SUMMER: delicate and muted, navy, mint, lavender

FALL: warm, intense, muted, orange, red, brown

WINTER: cool, intense, clear, ice blues, neon, metallics

3. What type of color scheme do you want? (Circle one.)

MONOCHROMATIC (one color and its shades or tints)

COMPLEMENTARY (two colors opposite each other on the color wheel)

SPLIT-COMPLEMENTARY (one color plus the color on either side of its opposite on the color wheel)

ANALOGOUS (one main color and up to six neighbors next to it on the color wheel)

4. Choose your base colors.

a. My basic white for trim and walls (if applicable) will have (circle one):

WARM UNDERTONES   COOL UNDERTONES

b. My default neutral will be (circle one):

WARM WHITE   BROWN   GRAY

BEIGE   COOL WHITE   BLACK

5. Choose your first, second, and (optional) third colors.

a. My main color will be _____

b. My second color will be _____

c. My (optional) third color will be _____

6. Choose a whole home general color scheme.

Throughout your house you can use your white, neutral, and chosen three colors in different proportions. For example, in your living room, you could use mostly the white and neutral with only hints of your main color in accent pieces like throw pillows. But in the bedroom maybe you want to use your main color with pops of your third color. Mixing the ratios of the same five colors (three colors plus your white and neutral) is how you create cohesive flow without every room looking the same.

Now, list the rooms in your house. Indicate what color the main color is or will be in each room. This could be your white or your neutral, or one of your three colors, and it could be used on walls, furniture, or accents. Then indicate which of your additional colors you will use to a lesser degree. (These are general colors. We will choose paint colors in a moment.)

ROOM	MAIN COLOR (60%)	SUPPORTING COLOR (30%)	ACCENT COLOR (10%)

ROOM	MAIN COLOR (60%)	SUPPORTING COLOR (30%)	ACCENT COLOR (10%)

7. Choose your whole home paint scheme.

Now I want you to choose paint colors that incorporate your selections on the previous questions and what you've learned. Remember to choose paint colors with your major furniture pieces or inspiration fabrics in mind. Never choose the paint colors first.

ROOM	TRIM COLOR	WALL COLOR	OTHER

ROOM AUDIT

Make copies of this worksheet and fill out one for each room of your house.

Room: _____

WHAT SPECIFIC ACTIVITIES WILL YOU DO IN THIS ROOM?	WHAT DO YOU NEED IN ORDER TO DO EACH ACTIVITY (FURNITURE, LIGHTING, OTHER)?	NEED?	HAVE?

WHAT DO YOU THINK OF . . .	LIKE?	DISLIKE?	WHY?
The shape of the room?			
Location of doors/ doorways?			
Location of windows?			
Architectural details or lack of?			
Location of immovable objects like fireplaces and built-ins?			
Existing colors on the walls, trim, ceiling, and floors?			
The amount of light in the room?			
General condition of the room?			
Other?			
Other?			

REPAIRS OR UPGRADES

DESCRIPTION	DIY OR HIRE OUT?	COST

BUDGET PLANNING

Make copies of this worksheet and fill out one for each room of your home. Then list the items you need for each room using the first section of the Room Audit worksheet as a guide. List the items in order of most needed/wanted to least needed/wanted. Research pricing for each item. Then list where you will get each item and its approximate price. Finally, total the cost for each room.

Room: _____

Budget: _____

ITEM	LOCATION	COST

CHAPTER 9

Step 3

Decorate One Room at a Time

So far we've taken a bird's-eye view and have identified your style and created a decorating plan for your entire home. This is where we switch gears and start to work on one room at a time. Where we plot the exact order to decorate it so that you will get results you love in each and every room in your house!

When God created the earth, He did it in a specific order. I mean, if He'd created man and woman before He created the atmosphere, Adam and Eve wouldn't have lived very long, right? Just as there was an order to the days of Creation, there's an order to decorating your home that works the best. The reason we decorate in the order I'm suggesting, though, isn't because it's the way designers do it. It's actually because after experimenting with it for years, this seems to be the easiest order for beginners to decorate their own spaces. Often the women I work with either via the blog or my design services can't visualize the finished space the way a designer would. They can't picture how an empty room will look with all the little details.

So, even though as you work on a room it may seem like a wee bit more physical work to do things in this order, I promise you it will make it so much easier for you to really *see* how things will look.

1. Choose a Room to Decorate, Get the Big Pieces, and Paint

Your budget and the priorities you have for your home will determine which room you will work on first. Sometimes for beginners, it's best to start small and tackle a powder room or small bedroom first to get your feet wet. Or, if you feel confident, you can jump right in and get started on the main spaces of your house. If necessary, go back and review all of your notes. Then choose which room you will start with! (So exciting!)

If any large pieces are needed for the room you've chosen, you need to get those pieces (with room measurements in mind). You should never choose colors, art, or smaller accessories until you have the necessary large furniture pieces in a space. If you have them in place, awesome! If you need to purchase them, that is what you need to use your budget on before you get into the rest of the things.

Once you have your major pieces, you need to create a blank canvas to allow yourself space to think. And you need to designate a holding space somewhere in your house where you can empty the room you'll be decorating.

Collect up all the tchotchkes, throw pillows, curtains, and other accessories and place them in your temporary holding space.

Clear off tabletops, shelves, and walls. Remove baskets, magazines, and plants. Do not leave any decorate-y knickknack, whatchamacallit, or bobble-thingy in the room!

Keep removing things until you have eliminated all the smaller and unneces-sary things from the room. Remove all the items that don't serve the current purpose of the room—as you defined it in the last chapter. No random side tables, no extra crates, zero miscellaneous accessories. Just the large pieces that are absolutely necessary to the purpose of the room. Things like the couch and side tables or the bed frame, mattress, and nightstands. Only the furniture pieces you decided the room absolutely needed when you defined the room's purpose get to stay in the space right now.

So many of us need quiet and a space devoid of visual clutter in order to think straight. I can visualize a room as its best self like nobody's business. But nothing helps me to be creative like the blank slate of an empty room.

An empty room (or at least a nearly empty room) means that you will have nothing to distract you. Your brain won't get stuck seeing what's there, what *is*, instead of what *could be*.

Now sit in the room and soak in the quiet for a few minutes. Or half an hour. You know, whatever. ;) Consider asking the Holy Spirit what the room does or doesn't need for the purposes and events that will occur there. Or just sit and be still.

Then, after soaking in all that quiet, if the room is not already painted the color you chose for it in the last chapter, paint the room yourself or hire someone to do it before moving on to the next step.

2. Furniture Layout and Space Planning Two Ways

Here comes one of my favorite parts of decorating . . . the room's furniture layout!

Method One

Now, when I say that we're going to be talking about furniture layout and space planning, with this method I don't really mean it in the way a typical designer would. Interior designers will measure a room and draw out the furniture, note all of the outlets, windows and doors, etc., and then map out the traffic patterns of the room before drawing a floor plan. Which is a great way to plan a room when you've been doing it for years and can visualize a space that way. But most people can't.

For beginners, I prefer to use a more hands-on approach. One that uses a little muscle power, but makes it very easy to visualize how the room will look. It's a method that allows you to move around in your space to view it from various angles and really get a feel for how the space will function for you. (Please enlist the help of a strong spouse or friend for this section if you are not comfortable or able to move furniture yourself.)

It's important to note again that your room should be mainly empty. The only things in the space should be the larger, purposeful pieces that you determined were necessary for the function of the room. No little bits and pieces, no accents. Not even any artwork or lamps! Just the big stuff.

The steps to planning a room layout this "easy way" are:

1. Identify the room's focal point

   You need to choose a focal point to decorate around. This is one of the most important things you can do in a room. If you have a focal point, and you keep the rest of the room simple, you will keep your space from feeling overwhelmed and chaotic.

   This is pretty easy if the room you're decorating has say, a large fireplace or picture window to orient the furniture around. The focal point is essentially chosen for you, like it is in my living room, with the fireplace on one end wall.

   However, it takes a bit more effort if there is no built-in focal point.

   Here are a few focal point ideas for you if you have to create one for yourself:

   - In a bedroom, the focal point could be the bed/headboard.
   - In a family media room (much to the typical designer's dismay), it could be the television.
   - In a dining room, the focal point would be the dining room table.

   When you think about each room, it should be fairly obvious

what or where the focal point should be. Choose your one—and *only one*—focal point for the room. If needed, move it to the best possible place if it's movable, so that when you walk into the room the focal point draws your eye toward it.

2. Arrange the furniture

Rearrange the large furniture pieces to suit the space around the focal point and for the current purpose of the room. You can bring in smaller accent furniture now. If the room is large, or has several purposes, set it up to include zones like a conversation area or somewhere to play board games, do puzzles, or read a book. Try to arrange everything so that the space feels open and welcoming—so you feel relaxed when you walk into the room. Often it helps to stand and look at it from a doorway as well as other angles.

Feel free to step back and look at the room as many times as necessary (and for as long as necessary) to decide if you've chosen a good arrangement. You want to love the space. Walk around to ensure you've left enough space for movement (see the space guidelines in the next section). Sit down and pretend to have a conversation or watch TV. If you aren't happy with how the room feels or looks, by

all means tweak the layout until it works for you.

And remember, more color, fabrics, and accessories all come later to fill and soften the room. Just focus on the function and the focal point of the space right now.

Method Two

If you wish to employ the typical space-planning method that designers use by putting together an actual pen-to-paper floor plan for your space, here's how:

1. Measure your room and draw it out on a piece of grid paper—one foot in real life equals one square on the paper scale.

2. Mark door openings, windows, floor registers, and electrical outlets.

3. Then measure and sketch your large furniture pieces on a separate sheet of grid paper. Rectangles and circles are good enough representations. You could also get a furniture template. Just be sure to use the same scale for your furniture sketches as you did for the floor plan. Cut those out and "rearrange" your to-scale paper furniture in your paper room until you are happy with the results.

4. Or draw the furniture on with a pencil. Erase and "rearrange" as necessary.

Here are a few guidelines to keep in mind when choosing your furniture layout:

- Keep 15 to 18 inches of space between a coffee table and a sofa.
- To keep traffic flowing well, there should be a minimum of 3 feet around the most prominent objects in the room, such as behind dining room chairs. Major walkways need 30 to 48 inches of space, but minor ones can get away with as little as 24 inches of space.
- You can safely use one oversized item in a room to add drama without making the space look crowded or cheap. But the other pieces should properly suit the scale of the room. Don't buy a matchy-matchy set of oversized couches and the coordinating coffee and end tables, for example. Scale can be very tricky. Employ an extra set of eyes if you need help with this.
- If you plan to watch television in the room, seating should ideally be placed away from the TV at a distance of three times the diagonal measurement of the TV. For example, if you have a 40-inch television, the seating should be about 120 inches away.
- If you have a small room, feel free to place the major furniture pieces along the walls, but avoid doing so if the room is larger. Placing at least one piece of furniture at an angle will go a long way to creating a designer look in your home as well.
- Symmetrical (basically two of everything in a mirrored layout) furniture layouts are easier for beginners but can look more formal than asymmetrical layouts.
- You will need access to electrical outlets for electronics, so be sure to keep them in mind when deciding on your arrangement. Of course, you can also use extension cords or power bars. (Always follow instructions and keep safety precautions in mind.)
- If you have to put a piece of furniture (say a couch or a bed) over a heat register, that may be okay. That's why they make special floor register vent covers that blow the air forward instead of straight up.

Regardless of which method of space planning you choose, just remember to choose a focal point and go from there. Make the space work for you given how the room needs to function (remember its purpose) and its focal point.

And never fear—you can always change the layout later if it's not working for you. You literally cannot mess this up in a permanent way!

3. Area Rugs and Window Treatments

Although it may seem counterintuitive and even a little crazy to place all the furniture and then choose a rug and window coverings, it is definitely the best way for a beginner to go about it. Yes, it's easier to put down the rug before there's furniture in the room. I totally get that. But until you know your furniture layout and which items are staying and which are not, you will not know what size rug to choose or how full the curtains should be, for example.

Area Rugs

Area rugs are great for warmth and noise reduction to reduce the echo in a room. Area rugs anchor the space and can define one or more zones in a large room. Of course they can also add a dash of style, pattern, and color too. And if you're renting or can't change your flooring, area rugs can go a long way in covering up floors you don't love.

AREA RUG MATERIALS What materials you choose for your rugs depends on the use of the space. For example, if you still have babies crawling around on the family room floors, a jute rug is not the best option as it will scratch their tender skin. Instead try shag, cotton, or a synthetic material.

Wool is a rather perfect material for rugs as it's quite durable and colorfast (it resists sun-fading, etc.). Yes, it does "shed" for a little while. But if you can just take five minutes to vacuum the edges of the room (where the little hairs tend to float to) a couple of times a week, I promise you will love a wool rug! If you can't commit to vacuum the little hairs for a short while, perhaps a different material for your rug would make you happier.

AREA RUG SIZING As for the size of the rug you need, that depends on the size of the room. You've got to get this one right!

ALL THE FURNITURE ON THE RUG

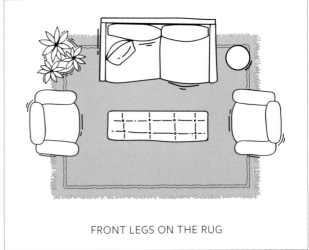

FRONT LEGS ON THE RUG

So many times an otherwise beautiful room is ruined (or at the very least made to look much less lovely) by a rug that is too small. Yes, large rugs cost more. But there are some great places to find them for less. And larger is better than too small. In a living room, for example, the rug should at least be large enough for all of the front feet of the couches and chairs to be on the rug. Use the area rug size guide below to help you determine the perfect size rug for your room.

LIVING ROOM AREA RUG OPTION 1 The most classic area rug sizing in the living room is to have all of the furniture entirely on the rug. You will need a rather large area rug, but the exact size will depend on the size of your furniture and the size of your room. This option is perfect for uniting a room that may not quite be entirely coordinated. A typical area rug size for this look in a living room is an 8' x 10' rug or larger.

LIVING ROOM AREA RUG OPTION 2 Another very acceptable option in the living room is to have a rug just large enough for the front legs of all of the furniture to rest upon. This works well in a slightly smaller living room or if you are on a tighter budget. A 5' x 7' area rug could work in this type of situation, but again, measure to be sure all of the front legs will rest on the rug.

DINING ROOM AREA RUG OPTION 1 In the dining room there are two common choices for area rugs. The first is a rectangular area rug. This will of course work best if you have a rectangular or oblong dining table. The most common rectangular dining room rug is an 8' x 10' rug. Anything smaller and you run the risk of the chairs not being on the rug. If you have an unusually smaller or larger table you may of course need a different size rug.

DINING ROOM AREA RUG OPTION 2 The second dining room area rug option is a

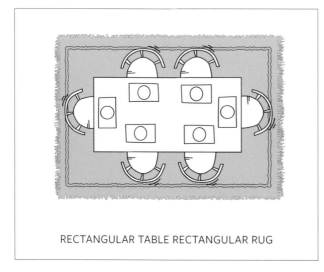

RECTANGULAR TABLE RECTANGULAR RUG

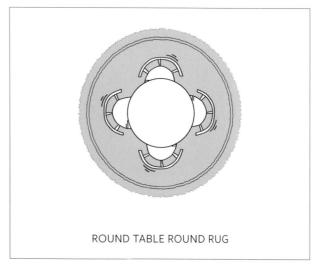

ROUND TABLE ROUND RUG

ALL THE FURNITURE ON THE RUG

JUST THE BED ON THE RUG

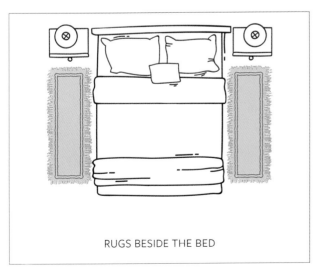

RUGS BESIDE THE BED

round rug to go with a round table. If you have a typical four-seater table, an 8' x 8' round rug is likely the best size for your room.

BEDROOM AREA RUG OPTION 1 With this version of area rugs in the bedroom, you need a rug that is about 8"–18" smaller than the length and width of the room. All of the furniture sits on the area rug, leaving only a border of bare floor showing around the edges of the room.

BEDROOM AREA RUG OPTION 2 With this area rug choice, the rug will peek out from under the bed, more so at the foot of the bed. Also, the rug won't extend all the way to the head of the bed and the nightstands will not sit on the rug at all. Typically an 8' x 10' rug will be perfect in this situation, but turned so that the longer side is parallel to the head and foot of the bed.

BEDROOM AREA RUG OPTION 3 If you'd like to keep the bedroom area rug budget to a minimum, this option is perfect. You can choose rug size based on the size of your bedroom, perhaps a 3' x 5' runner or even longer on each side of the bed.

AREA RUG COST As for the cost of area rugs, pricing can vary wildly from shop to shop. My favorite places to buy rugs online are Rugs USA and Wayfair. We've also had great luck with some larger rugs at The Home Depot and smaller ones from Homesense (Canada)/ HomeGoods (U.S.A.).

Online stores make it easier than ever to shop around and compare prices, so you should absolutely be able to find a rug you will love for a much more decent price than ever before.

AREA RUG TIPS

- Scotchgard your area rugs to prevent stains. Test in a small inconspicuous area first to be sure it won't damage the rug or change its color.

- If you have a puppy and don't want to have to buy a new rug because it's been chewing the edges, buy a spray called Bitter Apple. It comes in a red spray bottle and can be found at most pet stores.

Honestly, these two things were life-savers for our area rugs when our puppy Jackson was little!

Your area rug can be one of the patterned items that you pull your other colors from. So keep this in mind when choosing which area rug to buy.

Window Treatments

Window treatments are for privacy and style as well as warmth and dimming of noise (again, no echo-y rooms here!). What you choose to use as window coverings and adornments is entirely up to you.

In most of our last house, we used faux wood blinds for privacy and light dimming, and curtains/drapery for style. You can use both, use one or the other, or do

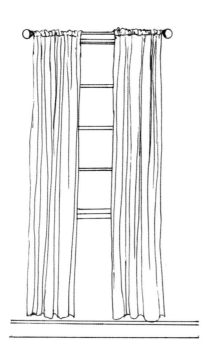

Hang curtains "high and wide" rather than crowding the window. A good rule of thumb is to hang curtain rods 3"–6" beyond the window frame and halfway between the top of the frame and the ceiling.

something entirely different—like California shutters or bamboo roll-up blinds. I do recommend curtains in just about all rooms except for bathrooms and kitchens. There's just something so beautiful about them!

Much like area rugs, curtains are often done wrong. More often than not, curtain rods get hung too low and the curtains themselves are often far too short.

So how long should curtains be and how high should you hang them? Curtains should be hung high and wide with a slight puddling on or "kissing" the floor. At the very minimum, curtains should reach the top of the baseboards in the room. A good rule of thumb to make a window look larger and to let more light in is to hang the rod 3 to 6 inches beyond the window frame on each side and halfway between the top of the frame and the ceiling.

Do you see how the sketch on the left makes the window look small and dark? And how the curtains hung high and wide on the right opens up the window and makes even this small glimpse of the room seem larger? Hang your curtains high and wide for the best effect.

BUDGET WINDOW COVERING OPTIONS If you're on a tight budget, there are so many inexpensive alternatives for window treatments. Here are just a few:

- Sheets or drop cloths hung with ring clips make very cost-effective decorative curtains.

- Ikea has a plethora of inexpensive curtains, in all colors and lengths. They do neutral colors and patterns especially well.

- You can use raw fabric with ring clips—simply fold, sew, or hem the edges with iron-on hem fuse tape.

- While curtain rods can be rather pricey (especially if you have large picture windows), they don't have to be. As I mentioned in the budget decor ideas section, you can also use painted pipe, dowel, or metal rod as curtain rods. Most big box or decor stores sell curtain rod brackets separately, so mounting these budget-friendly DIY rods is easy.

4. Lighting

After you've planned the layout of your room and added in the softening effect of drapes and area rugs, it's time to implement the lighting.

The Purpose of Lighting

You might think that the only purpose of lighting is to light a room. Somewhat obvious, yes? However, lighting is not just to illuminate a space. It can also be used to set a mood. Lamps, chandeliers, and other light fixtures all add a layer of style to a room as well. With the addition of dimmer switches, you can really create lovely ambiance in a room!

A QUICK SHORTCUT TO PERFECTLY COORDINATED COLORS AND PATTERNS

If you have a pattern in your furniture (like your couch, for example) you may wonder how to make all the furniture, rugs, and curtains work together. I have an easy solution for that:

- ▸ If your couch has a multi-colored pattern, then your other colors should be taken from that.
- ▸ If the larger pieces are not patterned, then use them as one of your solids or secondary patterns, and feel free to add pattern in the rug or curtains.
- ▸ Remember to use only *one* multi-colored pattern. Then you can use other single-colored patterns (like plaids, checks, and stripes with one accent color paired with white or your neutral) and solids in colors drawn from the multi-colored pattern. Use this formula at least until you are very comfortable mixing and matching patterns on your own.

In this way you can mix and match colors and patterns in a living room with the furniture, rugs, curtains, and even throw pillows, and also in a bedroom with the duvet, sheets, and pillows.

  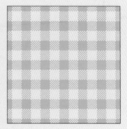

The Three Types of Lighting

There are three types of lighting for use in your home: general lighting, task lighting, and accent lighting. What are the purposes of each, you ask? Thankfully the names are rather obvious.

GENERAL LIGHTING General lighting is also known as ambient lighting. It provides overall lighting for a room to allow you to perform general tasks and to move around without bumping into things. *Examples of general lighting include chandeliers, wall sconces, table and floor lamps, as well as flush mount ceiling lights.*

TASK LIGHTING Task lighting helps you with certain tasks like reading, writing, or knitting. Task lighting can be achieved with track lights, table lamps, desk lamps, and/or pendant lamps.

ACCENT LIGHTING Accent lighting provides extra "oomph" and extra dimension to a room by accenting special features such as art, architectural features, and plants. *Accent lighting can be achieved with track lighting, wall mounted lights, or recessed lights.*

Didn't I tell you they were pretty obvious?

While you're working on each room, keep in mind that general and task lighting are necessary in all rooms and spaces, while accent lighting is optional.

Be sure you have adequate general lighting in the form of overhead lighting or table lamps as well as any task lighting necessary for specific activities that

Make sure you choose lamps that are the correct scale (bottom sketch) and not ones that are too small for your space (top sketch).

take place in the room. If you can install dimmer switches for your general lighting, you'll find that goes a long way to creating a cozy atmosphere.

Where Should You Shop for Stylish Lighting on a Budget?

The biggest secret to sourcing lighting for your home on a budget is to shop around and compare prices—especially online. I've often found that big box stores have a better selection *online* than they do in-store because they simply can't stock everything at all their brick-and-mortar locations.

Most of the lighting in our homes was purchased from The Home Depot, Wayfair, Lowe's, Joss & Main, or Birch Lane. And 99 percent of the time the lighting I bought was very budget friendly. I think I've splurged once or twice on something I've absolutely loved. But even a splurge for us was a couple hundred dollars for table lamps versus thousands that some designer companies charge for lighting.

With so many options at all price points, there's no reason to have ugly light fixtures! #banalltheuglylights

5. Walls and Art

Ah, the walls.

Wall decor comes after the furniture, rugs, curtains, and lighting because you won't truly know how much visual space you have until after those things are in place.

If you've been the good student I know you are, you have your major furniture pieces, area rugs, and window coverings in place and your walls already have their paint color on them. This decorating the walls section is just about adding any desired pattern and texture as well as some art to personalize your space, incorporate more of your style, and make your home even more of a reflection of you. There are so many options available to you when it comes to wall decor. I want to encourage you not to get overwhelmed.

Let's look at them one at a time—wall treatments first and then art.

Wall Treatments

Unless you already know exactly which wall treatments you want for this room—and you might—I want you to go back to your personal decorating style notes. What did the walls look like in photos of the style(s) you love? Were they plain and white? Were they shiplapped, stenciled, or planked? Were they wallpapered? Use these thoughts and observations as your guide to decorating your walls and choosing any wall treatments you may want.

I also want to remind you to only choose one to two wall treatments for each room. For example, choose white shiplap if you love that look, or choose wainscoting and wallpaper. But don't choose all three for the same room. It would be too much. Trust me on this!

Let's look at some wall treatment ideas.

TEMPORARY WALL DECOR OPTIONS Maybe you're renting right now or maybe you own your house but you're unsure of future plans. Or perhaps you're decorating a kid's room and you *know* things will change in a few years, so you don't want to commit to a major wall accent. Thankfully, there are a lot of temporary wall decor options these days.

Some options include:

- Washi tape crosses and other designs
- Removable or repositionable decals
- Painted accent walls
- Removable wallpaper
- Painted stripes or other patterns
- Stenciled walls

DIY AND OTHER WALL TREATMENTS If you know you're not going anywhere any time soon, or you don't have to work within the constraints of a landlord's rules, you can choose from an even larger selection of wall treatments!

Some of those options include:

- Wallpaper—all over or on a single wall
- Beadboard—full wall, half wall, or even on the ceiling
- Board and batten—full wall or partial wall
- Shiplap
- Other types of wood-planked walls
- Wainscoting

Once you've chosen the wall treatment you want to use, go for it! There are plenty of tutorials online. Put it up yourself or have someone help you. Keep in mind your room's focal point, and don't detract from that with your wall treatments.

You may have to move the furniture you've ever so carefully arranged while you complete your wall treatment. But I assure you it is worth it to do it in this order because you'll *know* that the wall treatment you're installing works in the space because you've worked in the room's essential elements first.

Bonus Tip: Take photos of your furniture layout before you move it to install your wall treatments so you'll know exactly where to put the furniture back afterward!

Art

Of course, another fun part of decorating a room is art. One thing to note is to never hang art until the curtains are up and the lighting is chosen and installed. This is because the placement and scale of your art would most likely be wrong once the curtains and lighting are installed and visually taking up space.

When choosing new art, it's good to have a look at your style notes and Pinterest boards again. Do your favorite inspiration spaces have colorful art or is the art black and white? Are there gallery walls or large individual pieces of art?

When it's time to select wall art, there are many wonderful options to choose from:

- Architectural salvage—shutters, corbels, gates
- Framed posters
- DIY canvas—lettered, silhouette, string art, abstract
- Large photos—blown up
- Maps
- Family photos
- Gallery walls

- Traditional paintings and pop art
- Scripture art (as we discussed in chapter 3)

You can make much of your art easily changeable by using clips on wire or hanging it with 3M Command products.

Art is another one of those things that's often installed incorrectly. Usually it's hung far too high. Keep in mind that

Be sure to follow the guidelines on the next page for art size and placement so that your art looks good in your space (bottom sketch) and isn't too small or awkwardly placed (top sketch).

larger pieces are better than pieces that are too small for the space, much like area rugs.

Here are a few guidelines to keep in mind when hanging art:

- When hanging art, keep its center at eye level, which is generally 56" to 60" from the floor. If you're hanging multiple pieces of art, keep the center point of the whole arrangement at this level.
- When hanging art above your sofa, make sure it's about 2/3 the width of the sofa.
- You'll also want to leave a maximum of 5 to 9 inches of space between the art and the top of the furniture. (See the illustration of this done wrong and then done well on the previous page.)

Once you've chosen the art you want to use, put it up yourself or have someone help you. You're getting so close to being finished. Now you're ready for the final finishing touches!

6. Finishing Touches and Accessories

The finishing touches are just that—touches. Because you've completed all the previous decorating steps, you will *not* need a lot of accessories for your room. You do not want to clutter up the room that you've worked so hard on, right?

Where to Add Accessories

Accessories can be added to any of the surfaces in your room, such as:

- Sofa tables
- Side tables
- Coffee tables
- Fireplace mantel
- Bookshelves

It's not necessary to place pretty things on all those surfaces, though! Make sure you leave enough space for people to set down a drink or a book. Plus, a little empty space is not a bad thing.

Adding Color and Trends with Accessories

Accessories are where I finally encourage you to add color and trends to your space. Of course, you should still keep in mind your personal decorating style and your whole home color scheme. But accessories are where I love to add the majority of color and trends in my house.

Adding color and trends with accents is the epitome of low commitment decorating. You want to be able to change accent colors should you tire of them, if the trends you're following change down the road, or even when the seasons change. If you implement your colors and trends with accents, there's little work involved and no big money to be spent if you want to switch out a few accents later on.

The finishing touches are items that are easily changeable and typically inexpensive. Especially if you comparison shop like the boss I know you are!

Here are a few of the accessories that you can use to add color and trends:

- Throw blankets
- Throw pillows
- Vases
- Flowers/Plants
- Photos
- Collections
- Antiques
- Objet d'art

The basic accessories that you want to add are

▸ A few throw pillows
▸ 1–3 vignettes or collections
▸ A centerpiece on a coffee or dining table

THAT'S ALL. You want a room that is finished but not overdone or cluttered.

In Canada, one of my favorite places to send beginner decorators for accessories is Bouclair. Bouclair stores are organized by color, so it's easy for newbies to just walk down a color aisle and grab a selection of coordinated accents to go with their color scheme! Maybe you could find a similar store near you that is organized by color. Or visit your nearest Homesense/HomeGoods and shop their aisles by color.

Elements of Design to Consider

The key to adding accessories well is in the details, and there are a few things you need to keep in mind before you go shopping for accessories or select them for each room from your stash.

SCALE Scale is one of the hardest things to get right and one of the things that amateur decorators mess up more often than not.

I don't remember where, but I once read that when you walk into a room it should resemble a cityscape—with a variety of heights and sizes. It's a good comparison. The secret to proper scale is a mixture of different shapes, heights, and sizes. One large item is better than many small items in most cases too, although you can cheat and create a vignette of smaller things that work together visually as one large item.

If you need another set of eyes on something to decide if it's the right scale, absolutely ask someone to help.

Another good way to determine the right scale and placement of decor is to take a photo and then study it. Somehow, a photograph really helps to see decor more clearly!

SHAPE To keep a room from looking sterile, make sure you have a variety of shapes. You should use at least one of each of the following shapes in your accessories and your vignettes: 1. Straight lines 2. Curves 3. Organic shapes (plants, flowers, hide rugs, raw-edge tables).

MASS When decorating with accessories (and even furniture) you need to pay attention to visual mass. Some pieces will look bigger than others even if they have the same dimensions. For example, a metal wire basket will take up less visual weight and space than, say, a solid wooden crate, even if they have the same dimensions.

Try to create visual balance with mass by varying your pieces.

TEXTURE Ah, texture. Texture is one of my absolute favorite elements of decorating.

Texture lends a room a certain character and coziness that would otherwise be missing. This is especially true when decorating with neutrals because texture keeps a neutral room from feeling flat and lifeless. Texture is often also the difference between a designer-looking room and a boring, so-so room.

Depending on your decorating style and the feelings you want to create in your home, you can layer on the texture with any of the following in your accessories:

- Woodgrain
- Tufting
- Tile
- Mirrors

- Pintucking
- Jute
- Lace
- Shag
- Sheepskin/calfskin
- Velvet
- Knits
- Lacquer
- Metallics
- Glass

OPPOSITES Decorating with opposites is another pro-tip you can and should use when choosing accent pieces. Opposites help to add drama and life to your rooms, something a little unexpected. Which is so much fun. Plus, opposites are a natural way to combine seemingly opposing decorating styles!

Examples of opposites that work well together include:

- Old and new
- Masculine and feminine
- White and black
- Matte and shiny
- Hard and soft
- Curved and straight lines
- Light and dark colors

Don't go crazy with opposites, but do try to implement at least one pair of opposites in each room.

Displaying Decor in Vignettes

A good trick to remember when adding decor is that accessories look much less cluttered and more purposeful if you create vignettes.

HOW TO CREATE A VIGNETTE Learning how to create a vignette is simple if you remember a few key things.

1. Create your vignettes on little-used surfaces like fireplace mantels or to one side of a sofa table or coffee table.

2. Use a lamp or other anchor piece as one of your items and build your vignette around its base. A lamp has the added bonus of illuminating the vignette when turned on at night.

3. Work with odd numbers. Three-item vignettes are the easiest to start with and are very pleasing to the eye.

4. Vary the height of the items. When using three items, for example, have a tall item, a medium height item, and a short item. Give smaller items needed height by placing them on a stack of books.

5. Create depth by building the vignette outward from back to front as opposed to lining the items in a row along the length of a surface.

6. Pay attention to the background. Vignettes often need a background to anchor them. A large mirror, photo, or framed piece of art work well.

GROUNDING VIGNETTES Vignettes are better than a scattering of accessories, but vignettes that are grounded or placed together on something are even better for beginner decorators.

You can ground a collection of accessories or a vignette by placing them on a:

- Tray
- Place mat
- Runner
- Mirror
- Cutting board
- Wood slab
- Picture frame
- Tile
- Book or stack of books

Grounding in this way is especially unifying when placing a decorative vignette on a larger surface like a coffee table or dining room table.

I also use grounding to keep items corralled in the kitchen or entryway. A collection of coffee-related items like the sugar bowl, creamer, and spoons becomes a handy makeshift coffee bar when placed neatly on a tray next to the coffee maker. Large utensils in a caddy and frequently used spices look very neat and tidy when collected on another tray by the stove. In the entryway, place a simple dish to collect discarded jewelry, coins, and keys.

Grounding is another designer level trick that you can employ to take your decorating to the next level.

How to Choose and Mix Throw Pillows

Along with vignettes, collections, and other decor accessories, you can add color, style, and even comfort to your decor with throw pillows!

Like the earrings of an outfit, throw pillows can complement and complete a room's look. They are also a fun way to play with color and pattern in a relatively inexpensive way! Especially if you shop around for them.

But sometimes it can be tough to know which patterns and colors go with which. You know, without creating a chaotic, messy look. Which is definitely *not* what we're going for, right?

An easy way to choose a combination of pillows is to simply lay pillows on the floor to see what goes well together. Add or subtract pillows until you get a mix you like. You can do this with toss pillows you already have at home, or even in the aisle at the store. (Shh, I won't tell.) Just keep in mind that the patterns and colors you've chosen in your furniture, area rugs, curtains, and wall treatments will need to play nice with the throw pillows you choose.

So, to recap the finishing touches:

- Accessories are where you should add color and trends into a space and where you can go with the trends if desired.
- Keep in mind scale, mass, shape, texture, and opposites when choosing finishing touches.
- You want to create 1–3 vignettes to display in your room. Alternately, you could display a collection instead of one of the vignettes (like a number of antique alarm clocks or several candlesticks).
- Use a base of some sort to ground your vignettes and collections.
- Throw pillows can be mixed and matched easily with the formula of one solid, one pattern, and one whimsical pillow. Repeat this for as many pillows as you need. Of course, keep in mind the other colors and patterns in the room.

The Necessity of Editing

So you've done it—you've got at least one whole room in your home decorated! Yay you!

One major thing to keep in mind when decorating with and buying accessories from now on is that you will need to *edit*.

Here's how to mix pillows effortlessly:

1 Pattern + 1 Solid + 1 Whimsical

▸ **Patterns** could be stripes, quatrefoil, trellis, floral, chevron, polka dots, plaid, paisley, scroll, gingham, damask, ikat, scales, or lattice.

▸ **Solids** could be any solid color in your palette *or* a miniscule pattern that looks like a solid from a distance.

▸ **Whimsical** examples are typographic words, sayings, mustaches, screen prints, photos, and watercolor.

You will simply fall in love with more things than you can realistically have in your home.

And just because you like it does not mean you have to have it. If you find you truly can't part with something or live without it, simply rotate your decor rather than having all your pretties out on display at once.

To help you to choose the right accessories, refer to the Decor Staples Checklist that's available on my website. Just go to HomeMadeLovely.com and type "decor staples checklist" into the search bar. It's a great resource to keep track of your wants and needs when shopping so you don't waste money buying things you don't need. It's also great for cleaning out a decorating stash and keeping only what you truly love!

Using the checklist, and closely examining what is still in your holding space from decorating this room, I suggest you donate what you don't love or need anymore. You don't need to hold on to what no longer fits your personal decorating style or color scheme.

I mean it. I want to encourage you to get rid of (donate to your local mission or thrift shop; sell on Craigslist, Kijiji, or Facebook Marketplace; give away to friends or family; throw away; or recycle) the remaining stuff that you removed from the room and aren't going to use again. Honestly, it's okay. Someone else may be able to use it. Someone else may even be looking for that very thing! It's just not for you anymore. Remember what I said about space back in chapter 4. You can only have as much stuff as you reasonably have space for.

Don't buy anything else without a purpose and a plan.

Remember, you will fall in love with more things than you can realistically have in your home. We all do. But if you really fall in love with something when you're out shopping, use the three-question purchase test below to see if the purchase is justifiable for you.

Three-Question Purchase Test

1 Does the item fit into the personal decorating style you've chosen for your home?

2 Does the item fit into your whole home color scheme?

3 Can it be used in at least *three* different places in your home?

If the answer is no to any *one* of these three questions, put down whatever it is and walk away.

A large part of decorating is editing, and *not* buying and displaying every single thing all at once. (That's also how you banish clutter from your house before it even begins to pile up!)

In the next section, we're going to talk about lovely hospitality in your home.

PART 4

WELCOME HOME

CHAPTER 10

Lovely Hospitality

IN ADDITION TO DECOR, I THINK a huge part of a lovely home is seen and experienced in how well and how often we welcome others in. Hospitality can be a wonderful gift for both the host and the guest. Loving on others through hospitality, feeding them, giving them a place to rest, and showing a genuine interest in what is going on in their lives is, well, *life-giving*. People are lonely and they want to connect. In fact, eating alone is more strongly associated with unhappiness than any single factor other than having a mental illness.[1]

Before I sat down to write this section of the book, I had to sort some things out in my own mind about hospitality. From chatting with friends, my own experiences, and those I remember as a child (and hearing my mom and her church friends talk about), I know that there can be a lot of guilt or "shoulds" associated with hospitality.

I spent the better part of a week praying through what to write on this topic of hospitality. I read several books entirely about hospitality. I searched for Bible verses that referenced hospitality. And I asked the Holy Spirit to clarify all of it so that I could lead you well in this area *without adding any pressure to your already busy life.*

After all that, I've come to believe that we get hung up on—and don't practice—hospitality for two overarching reasons:

1. Our hospitality doesn't look like we think it should.

2. Our homes have become fortresses.

Let's talk about how we think hospitality should look first.

Hospitality vs. Entertaining

One of my spiritual gifts actually is hospitality, even though I'm an introvert. (God totally has a sense of humor.) Because of that gift, I am entirely comfortable asking people over for a meal to love on them by serving their favorite foods and making them feel comfortable in my living room.

We know food sensitivities well in our own family, so I'm good with tough dietary restrictions. I keep decaf coffee on hand for my best friend in case she stops by because she doesn't do caffeine. I also keep throw blankets in a basket even in the summer, because my wonderful mother-in-law doesn't love my air-conditioning. We have five different kinds of sunscreen in a basket in case someone visits and has sensitive skin or needs a higher SPF. I keep a stack of beach towels in the main floor powder room all summer, just in case you forgot your towel and want to go for a swim. (I have yet to stock extra bathing suits though, so you best remember that!) I have a gazillion types of herbal tea for my herbal tea–loving friends, and I started keeping a supply of orange pekoe tea for my sister years ago, even though I don't like it at all. I have monogrammed mugs for just about every person I know, and if I don't have a letter when someone comes over, I usually order it for the next time they visit. I *love* to love on people in this way.

But I also work in an industry that exalts beautiful spaces and over-the-top entertaining. I spend a lot of time on Instagram and Pinterest for my business as well as participating in virtual home tours with very talented people. There are gorgeous layered tables for Thanksgiving, perfectly coifed Christmas trees where every ornament is oh-so-perfectly placed, and linen closets with labeled baskets and perfect little stacks of sheets and towels that never seem to get used. Perfect, perfect, perfect. I am surrounded by all kinds of styled perfection on a daily basis. And so are you if you're on social media. Unfortunately, all this striving for perfection has turned genuine hospitality into something it was never meant to be.

While I admire her, Martha Stewart's standards for hospitality and housekeeping are incredibly high. Much higher than I care to strive for. And actually, while the words *hospitality* and *entertaining* are often interchanged when discussing hosting people in our homes, they're really not the same thing at all.

In Martha's book *Entertaining*, she says, "Entertaining, like cooking, is *a little selfish*, because it really involves *pleasing yourself*, with a guest list that will coalesce into *your* idea of harmony, with a menu orchestrated to *your* home and taste and budget, with decorations subject to *your* own eye. Given these considerations, *it has to be pleasureful*"[2] (emphasis mine). Martha's idea of having people over is all me, mine, look at me!

This is the major signal that something is rotten in the state of Denmark. *Most of*

The difference between entertaining and hospitality is this: entertaining is all about the host and their home and "look at me," while hospitality is about obedience to God and serving and loving on our neighbors.

what is considered hospitality now is, in fact, entertaining, and not hospitality at all!

Along with the feelings of inadequacy if our homes or gatherings aren't Instagram- or Martha-worthy, are the very misleading feelings that we aren't doing hospitality as well as our Christian sisters. You know, the wonderful women who can bake pies (I literally once set the oven on fire trying to bake a pie and have baked only one since) and serve up three-course meals with ease. The women who have an open-door policy and always have time for coffee (without reheating it five times in the microwave before they get to drink it). Who consistently have dinner in the Crock-pot by 6:45 a.m. and never have dust bunnies blowing around like tumbleweeds. Who can make beans and rice seem like the most delicious meal on the planet. The ones who make even the Proverbs 31 woman look lazy.

But guess what? You don't have to do all those things. Or *any* of those things to practice hospitality. You really don't!

Aside from wrongly thinking we have to achieve some impossible level of perfection with our hospitality, there are all sorts of excuses we tell ourselves so we don't have to host: *I don't know how to cook, I'm too busy, we can't afford it, it's too hard with kids, my house isn't big enough.* And on and on we go, repeatedly talking ourselves out of just doing it already.

But in Romans 12, Paul lists the marks of a true Christian. Things like "Love must be sincere. Hate what is evil" (v. 9). And in verse 13 he says, "Seek to show hospitality" (ESV). In other words, showing hospitality is one of the outward displays of a Christian life. *It has nothing to do with making the perfect centerpiece or baking pies!* God can and will use you, right where you are, to love on those around you!

By focusing first on the Audience of One (God), the pressure is off. Hospitality becomes about welcoming and serving our guests. "Here you are" versus "Here I am." Serving others versus self-serving. "How can I love on you?" versus "Look at my shiny home." It's all about the heart behind the actions!

Home Should Not Be a Fortress

The second big reason we avoid hospitality is because current cultural views are that our homes are our private sanctuaries. Virtual fortresses where we retreat at the end of the day and lock ourselves away from the world to rest and unwind. And there's nothing wrong with that view, to some extent.

Occasional Netflix binges can be good for our weary hearts and brains. Naps in a quiet house should never be taken for granted. (Any other mommas want to say Amen?) And a meal with just your immediate family around the table can do wonders for communication and relationships.

We *do* need our homes to be a safe place for ourselves and for our families to recharge, away from all that the world demands of us. But, when our homes essentially become *idols* with this fortress mentality as the guiding force for how we live in them, and nary a friend or relative has crossed our threshold in months, that's a problem. One that I've honestly struggled with at times too. Especially in the middle of winter or when life is extra stressful and all I want to do is hibernate.

We were hardwired to do life together in community from the beginning. In Genesis 2:18, after creating Adam, God proclaimed, "It is not good for the man to be alone" and then He created woman. He created us to want and need each other. To be together. In New Testament times, Christian church togetherness also included hospitality and "breaking bread in their homes" with others (Acts 2:46 ESV).

You see, true hospitality is the exact opposite of the cultural views that we should separate and isolate in our little homemade fortresses. The authors of *The Simplest Way to Change the World* said it well: "Biblical hospitality chooses to engage rather than unplug, open rather than close, initiate rather than sit idly."[3] We love and wel-

come others because God has first loved and welcomed us.

So, how do we not barricade ourselves in our little castles and also not turn hospitality into some sort of perfection-seeking, selfish entertaining?

Come As You Are

One of the biggest things I love about the postmodern, post-Christian church world is the "come as you are" movement. Churches like the one we attend are actively working to create a new culture to welcome spiritually curious people in without some of the barriers that previously existed. Barriers that were part of my growing-up church life, like having to wear your Sabbath best or being perfectly groomed and proper. (My grown-up go-to-church outfit is jeans and a nice top paired with Birkenstocks or Converse All-Stars). The same attitude should be adopted for our hospitality. Not *only* for our guests, but for ourselves and our homes. Come as you are is good for hospitality. The authors of *The Simplest Way to Change the World* agree:

> The good news about hospitality is that it's not about image management—it's about sharing your real life with others. . . . In reality, you inviting others into your messy house is actually a beautiful act of vulnerability. It's letting them see that you are a busy, imperfect human who does not live in a glass house. . . . One of our friends suggested that the title of this sec-

tion should be "Jesus Doesn't Care about Your Messy House and Neither Do Your Neighbors and Neither Should You."[4]

I love that quote. *Hospitality is about sharing your real life with others.* Letting them know you're not perfect. Your table isn't perfectly set for a five-course meal, your linen closet is more than a little chaotic, and you've never managed to "properly" fold a fitted sheet in your life. You don't have it all together all the time. None of us do.

Now, before any wonderfully proper Southern ladies get mad at me, and think "bless her heart" to themselves . . . I'm not saying we should leave the laundry piled high on the dining room table when we know we have plans to have people over for dinner. Nor should we go to the store in our pajamas. I'm just saying we shouldn't be afraid to invite people into the midst of our real-life mess.

It's also important to remember that there are seasons in life. Mommas of young ones, *please really hear me here.* Sometimes you'll be able to clean from top to bottom and cook a three-course meal (if that's what you love to do) . . . but often you won't be able to do anything more than simply boil the water for a cup of tea. And that's OKAY! It's real and it's genuine.

Where Do You Start?

So, just where do you start with this biblical hospitality thing when you've either tried

and failed at it before or you have no experience with it at all? Well, breathe a huge sigh of relief, my friend, because you start right where you are, *with people you know.* That's right . . . with people you know.

You do *not* have to start by inviting the neighbors you've not yet met in for dinner. Yes, the Bible says that we should invite strangers in (Hebrews 13:2) and love on our neighbors (Matthew 22:39). And really everyone is our neighbor. But you can *practice* with familiar people first!

Once you've gotten the hang of loving on safe friends, family members, and fellow Christians, you can practice a little more with extended family or even people from work. They're still familiar, but maybe they push you outside of your comfort zone a little bit more than close friends do, either in beliefs or likes and dislikes and such.

Then, when you've practiced and have more of a handle on serving others with hospitality, you can move on to being hospitable with your geographical neighbors. You can even start with just coffee or lemonade on the front porch. That's right. You don't even have to invite people inside! Gasp! Most of our neighbors would likely prefer to get to know us outside a bit before they are comfortable coming inside our house anyway.

Ideas to Make Practicing Hospitality Easier

Not every event or dinner or coffee date you host will look the same. Nor should they. Biblical hospitality is about serving God and your guests, remember? Within your personal boundaries, hosting others can be open to prompting and life circumstances. Open to the day or week and the activities happening in your home and with your family. Here are some ideas to make going with the hospitality flow easier.

Invite Before You're Ready

Perfection is the enemy to *done*. It's also sometimes the enemy to *getting started*. If you wait until you *feel* ready to have people over, you may never do it. Ask God to help you focus on Him and the true reason you're opening your home to others. Ask who you should invite and what sort of hospitality to show them (fancy or simple, coffee or a meal). And then just extend the invitation! The act of obedience alone will be well worth the effort you put in.

Leave Some Margin in Your Schedule

This is good advice in general for us all in our busy, overscheduled culture. But it's especially true if you want to begin to practice hospitality more often. Depending on your personality, either leave some room for spontaneous invitations or set aside one day/evening every week or every other week to host people in your home. Call it Taco Tuesday, or Soup Saturday, or whatever you like.

I've begun to leave a little more margin in the unexpected area of my outdoor chores schedule. Cutting the grass at our house doesn't take long (our entire suburban backyard is pool and pool deck and the front yard is postage-stamp-tiny), which is why I sorta love it and don't assign it to anyone else's chore list. Because it doesn't take long, in the past I'd leave it for some wee pocket of time when I could run out, mow the lawn, trim the weeds, and rush back inside. But by leaving a bigger and more deliberate time slot for it, I've had room to spontaneously invite another mom in with her newborn for some motherly sharing and a cold glass of water on a hot summer day. And more than once this margin has left room for conversation with a neighbor I wouldn't have had the time to pursue if I'd been rushing to cram the job in before retreating inside again.

Leave some margin in your schedule for impromptu conversations. You'll be surprised by how well you can get to know your neighbors with these little chats!

No Adult Guests Upstairs Rule

We have a rule at our house (Jen Schmidt, author of *Just Open the Door*[5] has the same rule) and that's pretty much that there are no adult guests allowed upstairs. At our house, we don't say the rule out loud often, because we have a gate at the top of the stairs that's really tricky to open. It was put there to keep our dog from wandering through the bedrooms eating all the bobby pins and dirty socks. (Why does he do that?!) But it also effectively deters upstairs visitors. In practice, this rule means that we can always be ready for visitors by keeping the main floor relatively tidy. We can usually pick it up in about five minutes should someone drop by or text from around the corner to let us know they are on their way. And the main floor bathroom gets a lot more cleaning attention than the other bathrooms (it's spot cleaned as needed versus the other bathrooms, which are cleaned every two weeks). And no one is the wiser that at least one of our teenagers' rooms looks like a bomb went off. (Any guesses as to whose room that would be?)

Work with Your Introvert Tendencies

Like I said near the beginning of the chapter, I am 100 percent an introvert. That doesn't mean I don't like people. I do. It just means that unlike extroverts, who get charged up and energized by others, I get drained by people. But I know this, so I can still practice and enjoy hospitality by building in enough downtime or alone time to recharge.

I also don't have an open-door policy. That would wear me out, thinking I had to be "on" and ready all the time. Instead, I invite others deliberately. For years I've kept one day a week in my schedule as a coffee date day. During heavy writing or project seasons, these days were suspended for my sanity. (It's tough to keep a clean house when renovating or birthing a book.) But they were always added back in as soon as possible. And close friends know they can come anytime, but they need to text me first so I can pick up the living room and wipe down the powder room. (And maybe change out of my sweatpants.)

Don't let being an introvert stop you from loving on others. Just work with it by building in some downtime and setting some reasonable boundaries.

Be Prepared for Spontaneity

Yes, you can actually prepare yourself for spontaneity. One way I like to be prepared for last-minute guests—adults or kids—is to keep a few extra snacks on hand each week. Yes, any leftovers at the end of the week usually get eaten by hungry teens on grocery day. But for most of the week, there's something available to serve surprise or spontaneous guests. Like gluten-free quinoa cookies or Mary's crackers and hummus.

Of course, you already know that I keep plenty of coffee and tea and cold water on hand. And my Southern sister-in-law (whom I adore, by the way) taught me how to make sweet tea, so I can easily whip up a pitcher of that in a hurry on a hot day too.

The idea is to simply rethink your pantry and grocery list in light of practicing hospitality. You don't have to break the bank to be hospitable. You just need to think ahead a little bit and add a couple of extra items to your grocery cart.

Practice Scruffy Hospitality

I came across this description of scruffy hospitality online and I just love it:

> Scruffy hospitality means you're not waiting for everything in your house to be in order before you host and serve friends in your home. Scruffy hospitality means you hunger more for good conversation and serving a simple meal of what you have, not what you don't have. Scruffy hospitality means you're more interested in quality conversation than the impression your home or lawn makes. If we only share meals with friends when we're excellent, we aren't truly sharing life together.[6]

I want to encourage you to "offer hospitality to one another without grumbling" (1 Peter 4:9), and without any condemnation for how you have or haven't practiced it in the past. Romans 8:1 says that there is no condemnation in Christ Jesus. If you feel anything, let it be excitement at the thought that you can be hospitable with all *your* gifts and strengths, whatever they may be. Even if they don't include hospitality!

Start where you are. Make it easier on yourself by preparing. Remember the goal is not to show off your house or your gourmet cooking skills or to be selfish with your hospitality. The goal is to be obedient to God and to love your neighbor as yourself. The next chapter is filled with practical ideas to help you make this happen!

CHAPTER 11

Come On In and Stay Awhile

WITH THE DIFFERENCE between entertaining and hospitality in mind—*it's about them and not us*—we can create room in our homes for lovely hospitality to flourish. We can make our spaces more organized and prettier with the intention of creating a welcoming vibe from the moment our neighbors, family, and friends arrive at our doorstep.

Here are several ideas for creating that "welcome to our home" feeling from the curb appeal, into the entryway, and right through the rest of the house.

21 Curb Appeal Ideas Under $200

Great curb appeal can often be achieved with very little. Most of the following ideas are actually very inexpensive, with a few being only a bit more costly. Pick and choose what works for you in this season with your current budget. Keep other ideas in the back of your mind for later. And if you're renting, do whatever you can to increase your curb appeal, but don't stress about what you can't change!

1 Paint your front door. A small can of paint usually costs anywhere from $10–$20 but can really go a long way in sprucing up your front door. Choose a bold color that coordinates with your home's exterior to draw attention to your front entry. Or go with something more subtle to suit your personality and style.

2 Install a new doorknob. We've generally done this when we moved to a new house, especially if the knob has a lock. But you can do it anytime. And you can often find

clearance or discontinued knobs and handles at your local hardware store to get even more bang for your buck.

Add porch curtains. I have yet to do this, mainly because we have a small front porch and crazy winters. (Can you imagine the look of curtains frozen stiff from the winter wind and ice?!) But the look of pretty white curtains flowing in the breeze is welcoming—especially on a hot summer's day.

Lay out the welcome mat. Choose a large mat to stomp off the snow in winter, or layer your welcome mats for a more designer look. My favorite look is to place a large black mat on the bottom, with a buffalo check or plaid mat in the middle and a coir mat with a sassy or fun saying on top. (I've never quite gotten up the guts to buy the one that says "nice underwear" though.)

Switch out the mailbox for a more charming version. Or add one for packages and the paper, if you have community boxes like we do.

Hang a wreath. This is one of my favorite ways to add some curb appeal. You can find wreaths at all the major home stores and switch them out for a new look. Grab one for each

season and store them in the furnace room when they're not in use.

Install new house numbers. You can DIY your own or order one of those fancy personalized ones if you like.

DIY Wooden Shutters. I love shutters! Seriously. They're just so pretty, even when they're not functional and installed just for show. And they can be DIY'd for cheap too! Remember to seal them well for the outdoors, though, so you don't make your curb appeal worse instead of better with peeling, flaking paint!

If you have room, add a porch swing. Nothing screams come visit and share your day with me quite like a porch swing. Oh, how I wish I could do this. But, alas, our porch is nowhere near large enough for a porch swing.

Or a couple of cozy chairs. If you've got the space, definitely do this. Dean and I have even pulled out our folding lawn chairs a couple of times to sit out in front of our tiny porch. Neighbors always stop to chat when we do this.

Plant a tree. When we moved to this house the front garden was practically empty. (It literally had two dead mums sitting in it.) We added some easy-care black-eyed Susans and boxwoods surrounding a gorgeous vanilla strawberry hydrangea standard tree. That tree starts many conversations with passersby and even recently with the Swiss Chalet delivery guy!

Add a whimsical door knocker to show off your personality. You can get all sorts of beautiful knockers at vintage or architectural salvage stores. (And now you can all laugh because I said "knockers." Sheesh.)

Add potted plants to your porch, beside your garage, or hanging on pretty hooks. There's just something so welcoming about flowers and plants.

Add seasonal decor. This can be wreaths, inflatable Santas, scarecrows, or whatever floats your boat. We have one neighbor who has a blow-up Santa that's almost as tall as their two-storey house. You can be sure people notice and comment. Honestly, even if it's not designer worthy, who cares? If it makes the kids smile when they get to your house, I'm all for it.

Replace exterior lighting. I'm hoping by the time this book is printed, we'll have been able to do this. I never loved the twenty-year-old lighting that was here when we bought the house. But I have yet to find exactly what I want (or save up for whatever that is).

Flower boxes are so charming. Install them with a thriller, a filler, and a spiller. (Plants for impact, plants that fill in space, and plants that beautifully spill over the edges.)

Pressure wash the exterior of your house if it is looking a little dingy or sad.

Create a lovely pathway to your front door with pavers or rocks or anything, really. At one house we added flagstone. At another we added decking. Even just cleaning the weeds out of your existing pathway makes a huge difference in the welcome aspect.

Fly a flag. There are many options for garden flags. Everything from patriotic country flags to whimsical floral flags. Add a flag to your garden or fly one from your porch or garage.

Add landscape lighting. I adore the look of pot lights in the eaves, path lights, and garden lights. You can DIY your own or have someone come and install them for you, depending on your budget.

Apply stick-on vinyl welcome words to your front door. We had "hello" and "goodbye" on our last house's front door. At this house, on the outside of our double front doors, we have "hello" and "welcome." (Aside from welcoming our guests, they're a good reminder for me to be kind instead of annoyed when salespeople come to our door!)

A house's curb appeal is the first glimpse people get of your lovely home. It should be as welcoming and as lovely as you can make it. If you can create beautiful landscaping and a welcoming front porch, then by all means do that. But don't fret if you can't make it fancy. At the very least, in the daytime, try to make sure your walkway and porch are tidy and at night that they're well lit so no one trips on anything coming to your door.

10 Essentials for the Entryway

After the front of the house, our guests next see our entryway. No matter the size, you can make your entryway organized and welcoming with a few simple ideas.

If possible, add a few hooks reserved for guests. I don't know about you, but even with a nearby entry closet, our front entry tends to collect all our kids' stuff (and all my hubby's shoes). With a few hooks on the wall that are for visitors only, there's always a feeling of "Welcome, I was expecting you" instead of "Oh gosh, where do I put your stuff?" when people come over.

Keep a boot tray handy, especially for inclement weather. Otherwise, you may just find your entire entry is full of wet, melting snow and salt or dripping-wet rain boots. Yuck!

Try to fit in a place to sit down. Maybe a bench or even just a chair if space is tight. I know that the older I get, the more I and our even older guests appreciate not having to attempt to balance on one foot while putting a shoe on the other.

Keep a shoehorn handy too. We never thought of this until Dean's dad got older and needed one to get his shoes on. We picked up a nice long one at the dollar store and keep it tucked in the closet for when it's needed.

Lay down a pretty but tough rug. If your entry floor is tiled, this does double duty as something pretty and a means to stop slippage when the tile gets wet. Try to get something not too precious or expensive, though. Aim for durable material like jute or something that can be easily steam cleaned.

6 Hang a mirror. Everyone—*everyone*—likes to check how they look before heading out or after coming in on a windy day. Even if it's only big enough to check that your hair is not standing straight up and your mascara isn't running all over!

7 Hang a pretty light fixture—at the right height. (As I write this, we still have an entry light that is hung too low. So we're always telling our average height guests to watch their heads and our tall friends to watch their noses!)

8 Include small hooks or a tray for dropping your keys. We've had both in different seasons. Right now we have hooks for the spare car keys and the community mailbox key.

9 Tuck a lint roller in the closet or a drawer. It's especially handy if you have pets and you don't want your poor visitors (or yourself) heading out the door wearing oodles of dog or cat hair!

10 Hang art. This one is just for fun. But it can make an entryway look extra pretty.

These ideas are great suggestions, but you don't have to do them all. Much like the curb appeal section, you can choose the ones that suit your space and your style of hospitality.

5 Tips to Make Visitors Feel Extra Welcome

I love to make our guests feel extra welcome and loved once they're past the entryway too. Here are a few ways I've done that in the past:

1 Keep cozy throw blankets on hand for cool evenings (or for those friends who don't love your air-conditioning in the summer).

2 Stock up on monogram and saying mugs to make your guests feel extra special. Let them choose their initial or a fun sentiment that expresses their mood.

3 Keep a basket of extra socks or slippers near the door in case anyone finds your floors cold.

4 Have fun wine charms on hand so no one mixes up their drinks. (That's just embarrassing and totally icky during cold and flu season.)

5 Keep lots of ice in the freezer for friends and family who love their drinks extra icy. (Ahem, Mom and Megan.)

12 Good Ideas for Overnight Guests

Although we do have a guest room at this house, overnight guests are not an everyday occurrence around here. Well, they almost are if you count the teenagers that often stay over on the weekends! But they're treated more like our own kids, since it's generally the same handful of kids that are here frequently. They get their own bedding (a fitted sheet and a sleeping bag) from the linen cupboard and grab their own snacks from the pantry.

But adult overnight guests get slightly different "service" . . . a pretty made-up bed, extra toiletries, something to read, and a few extra comforts of home. Here are a few ideas for your overnight guests.

Keep extra toiletries on hand. We do this for our own family—things like toothbrushes and toothpaste—but we keep a separate stash for our overnight guests just in case. Things like soap, shampoo, conditioner, hairspray, and travel-sized (spray on) deodorants.

Have a variety of reading materials for guests. Sometimes when we sleep at a new place, it can be hard to fall asleep. A different mattress, different surroundings, and different food all contribute to difficulty drifting off. Having something for your guests to read could make this easier for them.

Provide some sort of white noise for your guests. Along with the above, sleeping in a new space can be hard because of different noises. So try to have a fan available that can be turned on for white noise and to block out those unfamiliar nighttime sounds.

Have a couple extra sets of towels (face cloth, hand towel, and bath towel) on hand that are just for guests. They won't get worn out as quickly as your everyday towels and will make your guests feel special and welcome.

If you have a dedicated guest room, make sure you stock it with things they may need, like extra pillows, an extra blanket, and Kleenex. If you don't have a dedicated guest room, you can still keep these things in a basket or closet to pull out when guests arrive.

Always put clean sheets on the bed. I probably don't have to say this, but just in case someone doesn't know it, this is a necessity! No exceptions!

Have somewhere to charge phones overnight. Either a visible and accessible electrical outlet or an extension cord near the nightstand will help.

8 Also have a place to set a glass of water. I know we're all trying to move away from single use plastic, so we don't often have bottles of water available anymore. Try to have a good spot to set down a glass of water for your overnight guests. Away from electronics is best.

9 Plug in a nightlight or two. You may choose to have one available in the guest room. But I generally just try to make sure there's one or two between the guest room and the bathroom, for those middle of the night trips.

10 Display the Wi-Fi password. Even if your guests get this from you when they arrive, technology can be weird. Make guests more comfortable by posting the current Wi-Fi password in their room so they can reconnect when necessary. There are loads of free printables on Pinterest, and even a few fancier signs on Etsy. Or you could use a letterboard or chalkboard to write the password on.

11 Provide a blow dryer if possible. This doesn't matter too much if your guests are sharing a bathroom with you and you have one in there already. But if your guest room is on a different level or is near a different bathroom, providing a blow dryer is super helpful!

12 Hang a mirror. There's nothing more embarrassing than waking up as a guest and not knowing that your hair is standing straight up or that you still have sleepy gunk in your eyes when you come to breakfast. Give your guests a mirror so they can at least take a quick look in the morning.

Incorporate some of these ideas to make your overnight and occasional guests feel at home while they visit—even if you don't have a dedicated guest room and they're staying in spaces your family uses 365 days a year.

Other Ways to Make Guests Feel Welcome

You can make your guests feel comfortable by writing friendly welcome greetings or seasonal sayings on letterboards, white boards, or chalkboards. You can also make them feel at home by making necessities like coffee and tea easily accessible and fun. I've got two DIY tutorials to help you with that—a DIY Coffee & Tea Bar and a DIY Chalkboard!

DIY COFFEE & TEA BAR

A temporary or permanent coffee bar or area in your kitchen is a lovely way to allow guests to feel welcome. Because a coffee & tea bar keeps things pretty and in plain sight, your guests and family can help themselves and have fun in the process.

SUPPLIES

- Coffee maker that takes pods
- Assorted coffee and hot chocolate pods (decaf and regular)
- A kettle
- Assorted teas (decaf and regular)
- Sugars, syrups, and other sweeteners
- Creamers or various milk options
- Mugs (and tea cups if desired)
- Spoons
- Spoon rests

INSTRUCTIONS

1 Decide on a location for your coffee and tea bar that makes sense. Keep in mind fridge space and access for creamers and milks, storage for extra coffee and tea, electrical outlets, and traffic flow.

2 Set up your coffee maker and kettle first.

3 Next, choose where you will keep your mugs handy. Will it be in a cupboard or open shelf above, or on a mug rack beside the coffee maker and kettle?

4 Stock your coffee and tea. Use baskets, shelves, or drawers to keep them organized.

5 Assign your sweeteners a place nearby. I like to keep mine in plain sight on the counter, but corralled on a tray.

DIY CHALKBOARD

Welcome guests, jot down the menu for the evening, or just leave a friendly message! Chalkboards are so much fun and make great versatile decor and hospitality pieces.

SUPPLIES

- One 4′ x 8′ sheet of half-inch thick MDF (medium-density fiberboard)
- Two 1″ x 4″ by 8′ pieces of pine
- Chalkboard paint (color of choice, I like classic black or even green)
- 1 foam roller
- 1 foam brush
- Stain (I used Varathane oil-based stain in Briarsmoke)
- Lint-free rag
- 16 – 1″ flathead screws
- Drill or screwdriver
- Hanging brackets (like saw-tooth hangers)
- Hanging hardware

INSTRUCTIONS

1 Cut the MDF to 36″ x 52″.

2 Next, cut each piece of the pine into one 52″-long piece and one 29″-long piece.

3 Using a foam roller, paint the MDF with chalkboard paint. You will need to paint one surface and all the edges. You do not need to paint the backside. Let dry and repeat. Follow the instructions on the label of your chalkboard paint for how many coats you need and dry times.

4 Using a foam brush, apply stain to all sides and edges of one piece of pine. Let sit for a moment, depending on how dark you'd like your stain to be. Then wipe off with a clean, lint-free rag. Repeat for all four cut pieces of pine. Let dry according to the package directions. (Also, dispose of your brushes and rag according to the package directions to avoid spontaneous combustion.

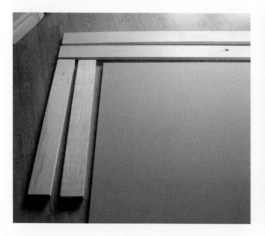

There's nothing like happily creating a DIY project and then blowing up your house in the process!)

5 Once your MDF chalkboard and pine frame pieces have all dried and cured (again, follow package directions), it's time to assemble your chalkboard. To do this, lay your frame pieces facedown on a table in the frame shape. Then place your chalkboard on top, facedown. Use clamps to keep everything in place, if needed. Screw the frame pieces to the chalkboard from the backside of the chalkboard, using four screws for each frame piece. When you affix the screws from the back of the chalkboard, they won't show on the front.

6 Attach your hanging brackets to the chalkboard.

7 Hang your chalkboard where desired with the appropriate hanging hardware for your walls.

8 To use your new chalkboard, first rub the side of a piece of chalk all over the surface. Then wipe with a dry paper towel or chalkboard brush. This should keep your chalkboard from having ghost impressions after you write and erase something. Write your message and enjoy!

CHAPTER 12

Gather around the Table

IF YOU GOOGLE THE SAYING "A family that eats together, stays together" you will get no less than 284,000,000 results. (Can you tell I like to Google things?) And if you skim through those results, you will find that most of them extol the benefits of family mealtimes. Of course, no true home is complete without shared food. It's been this way since the beginning of time. Eating together helps families to bond and build good communication. Sharing the table with guests as you practice hospitality is also an incredibly important facet of creating a lovely home.

Daily Family Meals

We have made it a priority for our entire family life to at least have dinner together every night. Dean leaves for work really early, and I am not a morning person, so once the kids could adequately get their own breakfast, weekday breakfasts sort of became a help-yourself deal. Lunches sometimes too, although for their homeschool years, I tried to get all the kids together for lunch every day. Dinner became the meal we all ate together. Some nights it was a long, lingering affair around the dining room table, complete with devotions and chatting. Some nights it was a shorter meal with less conversation and everyone rushing off to do their thing immediately after swallowing their last bite (and putting their plate in the sink instead of the dishwasher again). Ever so occasionally, dinner was a quick bite around the kitchen island, with the living room TV on because everyone was just too exhausted to chat.

Eating as a family helps to improve family communication, grades, social skills, eating habits, and sports performance, and it saves money versus picking up something less healthy from the drive-thru.

But it's not always easy to do dinner together. The fact is, the very same articles that say how important it is to eat together as a family, also say how much harder it has become to do this because of over-burdened schedules. We know plenty of families that have to go in at least three different directions each weeknight for all the kids' activities. And I get it. It's hard to say no. We want our kids to have all the experiences and learn as much as possible. Dance, hockey, soccer, gymnastics, piano, Scouts, and *all the things*. They're good things. But when they come at the expense of family togetherness, I have to question the validity of the experiences and the busyness they bring.

Just as when we decorate and have to edit and not buy things we like but don't need, when we set our families' schedules we need to prioritize. There will always be things vying for our time and our attention. We are to model our lives after the life of Jesus. Somebody was always wanting something from Him, vying for His attention—healing, hope, miracles. Yet, He made time for gathering around the table with His disciples and others all the time. He lingered at the table on many occasions. And we need to do the same. It's our job as parents to set the rules and expectations. In our family, we set the expectation that dinner was a family affair every day—with rarely an exception. Of course, schedules are drastically changing as our kids grow into adults and go off to college and get jobs of their own, but I hope and pray the habit of eating together is one they hold on to.

What on Earth Do You Feed Everyone?

It's not just our family that eats here. We frequently have a basement full of teenagers, a houseful of family for a holiday, or a once-a-month gathering of our small group spread throughout the house. And if you and I are practicing hospitality as we ought, that's just how it should be.

But how do we do it well? How do we make the most of our time and budget when it comes to meals and food for larger gatherings?

If cooking comes easy to you or it's something you're naturally good at, you probably already do the things I'm going to suggest. But if you're just starting out, or cooking really isn't your forte, here are some suggestions for how to gather people around your table without breaking the bank.

Meal Planning

Meal planning is essential in our house. We have three kids. I run a business from home. Dean works in the city. We homeschool. Everyone has different likes and dislikes when it comes to mealtimes. We even have a few food allergies and intolerance issues. When I fly by the seat of my pants and don't plan out our family's meals, we tend to eat out, which isn't good for us. And we spend more on groceries because we pop into the store just to pick up a cooked chicken, a frozen (dairy-free, gluten-free, expensive) pizza, or some other quick no-prep something, which always leads to just one more thing in the cart. The next thing we know we're way over budget for the week. Also, Dean and I tend to gain weight when I don't meal plan. Bummer.

But when I plan our meals for the week, it's almost magic! We keep the grocery budget down. We eat healthier. And I'm happier all around because I'm not panicking over what to make everyone for dinner. (Or that we just dropped $60–$100 or more on another unplanned dinner out!)

To help keep our family organized, I like to gather recipes, make lists, and plan out every meal for a week's worth of eating. I keep a running list of master meals and a running grocery list each week. Everyone is supposed to checkmark the list when they use the last of something. That works about 80 percent of the time. To compensate, I ask around on grocery day if anyone ran out of or is running out of anything.

Basically my meal planning process goes like this:

1. Check the freezer and pantry to see what we have.
2. Check our master meal lists to see what everyone likes.
3. Start writing meals onto the menu/meal planner sheet for the week, starting with meals that use ingredients we already have on hand.
4. Jot down items we need from the store as I go.
5. Completely fill in meal planner for all meals and snacks.
6. Post the meal plan somewhere easy to see like the fridge or the bulletin board.
7. Buy groceries. (And adjust meal plan if something needed wasn't available.)

Other things to include in your meal planning to make room for spontaneous hospitality:

- Shop meat sales to have roast or chicken stocked up in the freezer in winter
- Buy extra burgers and buns for last-minute summer barbecues
- Keep boxed cake mix (gluten-free) on hand in the pantry to make cake, cupcakes, or even quick muffins.

Meal planning helps to keep me sane during the busy week and sometimes lazy weekends.

Quick Muffins: Mix one box cake mix with one can pumpkin puree (no other ingredients). Scoop into muffin tins and then bake according to the box cupcake instructions.

Serve Just Drinks and Snacks

There is absolutely nothing wrong with inviting people over just for drinks. A pitcher of cold iced tea on a hot summer's day is the perfect thing to share with your neighbors to cool down. Or maybe a few mugs of hot chocolate will hit the spot after a marathon snow shoveling session in the middle of winter.

You could add in some super easy snacks like store-bought chips and salsa, or homemade cookies, if that's your thing. (I can't bake cookies to save my life. Squares and apple crisp, sure. Cookies and pie, not a chance! But my girls make the best gluten-free chocolate chip cookies ever!)

It doesn't have to be fancy to be hospitable, memorable, or special.

Budget-Friendly Snack Ideas

We have a Costco membership mostly for buying meat and snacks (and pool chemicals). We regularly buy healthier granola bars, salted almonds, other nuts, ginormous boxes of crackers, fig newtons, and quinoa cookies to keep on hand for the teenagers and other guests. Fruits and vegetables work as budget-friendly snacks but don't tend to hold hungry stomachs for long, unless they're paired with some sort of nut butter or hummus. We also buy lots of rice crackers each week, along with large jars of dill pickles, gluten-free cereal (with less than 9 grams of sugar per serving, and on sale whenever possible), almond milk, and bean chips.

Keeping a master snack list handy while meal planning helps to keep this grocery line item from getting carried away. We steer clear of most single-serve, individually packaged "fruit" snacks, cheese and crackers, or other snacks that are marketed for kids' lunchboxes.

Because of food intolerances, we probably spend more than some people do for this category. But the ideas above help us to spend less.

Make It Potluck

If you want to begin to have people over more often and either your budget is tight or you're not the world's best cook, you can go with the age-old favorite—a potluck. Depending on the number of people you invite and expect, you can either go all wild and tell everyone to bring what they want for a crazy smorgasbord of food, or you can assign certain people to bring certain things. Like all the single people bring salad and/or dessert. Or those with a last name of A–G bring a side dish and H–M bring an appetizer. You get the idea. You can structure it anyway you like. The key is to lighten your load and have everyone contribute to the fun.

Telling guests to bring enough for themselves and one extra person is a good potluck rule to ensure there's enough food to go around.

Have a Few Go-To Recipes in Your Arsenal

If you want to cook for your guests, then by all means do that. Having a few go-to favorites in your back pocket will certainly help make hosting easier.

By the time this book goes to print, I will have been married to Dean for twenty-four years and our oldest child will be twenty! That's a lot of meals prepped in two decades, many of which I can now make without glancing at a recipe. A few of those are ones I can whip up to feed a crowd or pack up to take to a potluck, or even deliver to a friend who needs it. Many of them are on my blog, but I'm including a few favorites here.

CREAMY COLESLAW RECIPE

We love to make this coleslaw to pair with pulled chicken made in the Crock-pot for Sunday lunch after church. Serves 6–8.

INGREDIENTS

- ½ head green cabbage, or a mix of green and purple*
- 2 large carrots*
- ½ medium red onion
- ½ cup mayonnaise
- 1 tbsp white vinegar
- 1 tsp white sugar
- 1 tsp celery salt
- black pepper, optional, to taste

INSTRUCTIONS

Peel carrots and trim off ends.

Using the grater attachment, process cabbage, carrots, and red onion in a food processor, then place into a large mixing bowl.

In a small mixing bowl, whip mayo, vinegar, sugar, celery salt, and pepper together.

Pour sauce over cabbage mixture and stir well to coat.

You can use bagged coleslaw mix instead of cabbage and carrots in a pinch to make this extra super-fast!

Shannon Acheson

CROCK-POT PULLED CHICKEN

A seriously easy recipe! We like to serve this pulled chicken with buns or over rice with a side of Creamy Coleslaw. It makes the perfect Sunday after church lunch. Serves 5–8.

INGREDIENTS

5–8 chicken breasts (fresh or frozen)

1 bottle of BBQ sauce (I use Kraft Original)

1 regular sized can of Pepsi (or Coke if you're a Coke person)

INSTRUCTIONS

Spray Crock-pot with non-stick cooking spray.

Add chicken breasts to the pot.

Pour BBQ sauce over chicken.

Pour cola over the chicken.

Cover and cook on high for 4 hours or low for 8 hours.

Before serving, shred chicken with a knife and fork or two forks.

CHICKEN POT PIE *with* QUICK SPOONED-ON CRUST

Don't have time to mess with pastry for a crust? Try this chicken pot pie with quick spooned-on crust recipe any night of the week! Serves 6–8.

INGREDIENTS

For the Filling

1 tbsp	melted butter
1 tbsp	rice flour
2 cups	chicken broth
½	onion, diced
3	carrots, peeled and diced
3–5	potatoes, peeled and diced*
1 cup	frozen peas or green beans (or a mix)
1–2 cups	leftover cooked chicken, cubed/shredded
1 tbsp	sage
½ tsp	sea salt
1 tsp	oregano
½ tsp	paprika
½ tsp	pepper

For the Quick Spooned-On Crust

1 cup	rice flour
1 ½ tsp	baking powder
½ tsp	salt
1 cup	milk
½ cup	water
1 tsp	vinegar
½ tbsp	melted butter

INSTRUCTIONS

In saucepan over medium heat melt butter.

Once butter is melted, begin to stir in rice flour a little at a time. Continue adding flour until butter and flour become a paste (roux).

Then whisk in broth a little at a time, allowing sauce to thicken before adding more broth.

Add the rest of the filling ingredients and stir over low heat until thickened.

Pour into a 9" x 13" glass baking dish, set aside.

Mix crust ingredients together in a large measuring cup or a bowl.

Spoon on or pour over filling.

Bake at 350 degrees for 30–45 minutes, or until crust is light brown and pot pie is bubbling. Serve warm with a salad, dinner rolls, or garlic bread.

*Potatoes can be substituted with sweet potatoes or more of the other veggies if desired.

SLOW COOKER ROAST BEEF DINNER *with* GRAVY

Roast beef is a classic filling and nutritious supper. This slow cooker roast beef dinner recipe is extra simple because the roast is cooked in the slow cooker from frozen! Serves 6–8.

INGREDIENTS

One	1.5–1.8 kg (3–4 lbs) beef roast
One	454 g, approx. 16 oz bag baby carrots
8–10	potatoes
½	red onion
One	900 ml (approx. 32 oz) carton beef broth OR 4 cups water
¼ cup	red wine/cooking wine/ sherry
1	bay leaf
1 tsp	each rosemary, sage, savory, thyme, and salt
1 tsp	Worcestershire or HP sauce

INSTRUCTIONS

Spray slow cooker with non-stick spray or olive oil.

Cut potatoes into 1–2 in. pieces.

Cut onions into chunks. (I leave mine large to add flavor and allow the kids to pick around them!)

Place roast in center of slow cooker.

Surround roast with potatoes and then carrots.

Top with onions.

Pour beef broth or water and wine/sherry over everything.

Submerge bay leaf into liquid.

Sprinkle with herbs, spices, and Worcestershire/HP sauce.

Cover and cook until roast is cooked through—on high for approximately 4 hours or low 8 hours.

Remove the roast and cut. Serve with veggies and gravy.

To make the gravy

INGREDIENTS

1 tbsp	butter or substitute
2–4 tbsp	rice flour
1 cup	broth—beef, chicken, or vegetable
	salt and pepper, optional

INSTRUCTIONS

In saucepan over medium heat melt butter.

Once butter is melted, begin to stir in rice flour a little at a time. Continue adding flour until butter and flour become a paste (roux).

Then whisk in broth a little at a time, allowing gravy to thicken before adding more broth.

Add salt and pepper (optional). Serve over roast and veggies.

BROCCOLI BACON SALAD

A serious crowd pleaser because it's a little sweet and a little savory. I bring this to just about every small group meal! Serves 4–8.

INGREDIENTS

- 1 head broccoli
- ¼ cup shaved carrot
- ½ medium onion
- ¼ cup sunflower seeds
- 1 cup mayo (I use a vegan mayo because eggs disagree with me)
- 1 tbsp white sugar or honey
- 1 tbsp vinegar
- 6 slices bacon (I use turkey bacon)

INSTRUCTIONS

Fry bacon till crispy. Remove from pan and set aside.

Cut broccoli into bite-size pieces.

Dice onion.

In a medium bowl combine all salad ingredients.

Mix mayo, sugar or honey, and vinegar together and pour over salad.

Mix till combined.

Refrigerate for 1 hour and then serve cold.

BLT PASTA SALAD

My kiddos LOVE this salad, and we often eat it for lunch. You can add avocado chunks and cooked chicken to make it more filling. Serves 4–8.

INGREDIENTS

- 1 lb noodles of choice, cooked and drained (I use quinoa pasta)
- 4 slices cooked bacon (I use turkey bacon)
- 2 tomatoes, diced
- 1 ½ cups romaine or head lettuce, thinly sliced
- ¼ red onion, diced
- 1 green onion, diced
- ½ cup mayonnaise (I use a vegan mayo because eggs disagree with me)
- ½ tsp dried dill
- 1 tsp kosher salt
- 1 tsp ground black pepper

INSTRUCTIONS

In a large bowl, combine the cooked noodles, bacon, tomatoes, and lettuce and toss.

In a smaller bowl, combine the mayonnaise, dill, salt, and pepper. Whisk together and pour into the large bowl.

Stir until everything is evenly coated and serve! Top with extra bacon, lettuce, and tomatoes if desired.

KOREAN BEEF BOWLS

Oh my gosh! These Korean beef bowls are soooo delicious and easy to prepare! And you can place the elements separately on a plate for picky eaters! (Ask me why I know that.) Serves 4–6.

INGREDIENTS

600 g	(1 ⅓ lb) ground beef
3	cloves of garlic, minced
¼ cup	brown sugar
¼ cup	coconut aminos (soy-free soy sauce substitute)
1	squirt sriracha
2 cups	baby spinach
2 cups	rice
2	avocados, sliced
2	green onions, chopped
	sesame seeds, optional
4–8 tbsp	sriracha mayo*

INSTRUCTIONS

Brown ground beef in a skillet or wok. Drain any excess grease from pan.

Add garlic to pan and cook, stirring, until fragrant.

Mix brown sugar, coconut aminos, and sriracha together and pour over cooked ground beef and garlic in pan.

Cook until heated through.

In individual bowls layer spinach with rice.

Add cooked Korean beef on top of rice.

Place avocado slices on top, to one side of beef bowls.

Garnish with green onions, sesame seeds, and sriracha mayo.

....

*I make my own sriracha mayo by mixing 3 tbsp of mayo (soy-free for me) with a couple of squirts of sriracha and about a teaspoon of water.

HOMEMADE HAMBURGER HELPER

Pure comfort food, in a hurry, without any bad stuff! Our home-made hamburger helper recipe is simple to make and tastes great! And it can be made dairy-free and gluten-free too! Serves 6–8.

INGREDIENTS

.5 kg	(1 lb) ground beef
454 g	(16 oz) spiral rice pasta
1 tsp	each paprika, oregano, parsley, salt
¼ tsp	pepper
1 tsp	Dijon mustard
3	cloves crushed garlic
1 cup	beef broth
1 cup	milk of choice (almond, cashew, soy, or rice)
½ cup	cheddar-flavored Daiya, or other non-dairy grated cheese substitute

INSTRUCTIONS

On medium heat, brown ground beef in a large skillet until no longer pink. Drain off fat.

Meanwhile cook pasta according to package directions. Strain and set aside.

Add spices, mustard, and garlic to cooked meat in skillet. Stir.

Carefully pour broth and milk into skillet. Stir to thoroughly combine with meat and spices. Add cheese and stir to combine.

Add pasta and stir to coat.

Cook until heated through.

MY MOM'S APPLE CRISP

Apple crisp is a classic North American dessert that can be made in a hurry and with imperfect apples. Delicious served warm on its own or with ice cream (or ice cream substitute). Plus, even horrible bakers like me can't mess it up! Serves 8.

INGREDIENTS

6–10	apples, peeled, cored, and sliced
½ cup	brown sugar
1 tbsp	flour
1 tsp	cinnamon, or more if you happen to be making it *for* my mom!
¼ tsp	salt
¾ cup	flour or rolled oats, or a combination
1 cup	brown sugar
¼ cup	butter melted, or oil

INSTRUCTIONS

Combine first five ingredients together and place into a greased baking dish (glass is best). Set aside.

Combine last three ingredients in a small bowl.

Sprinkle over apples, covering apples completely.

Bake at 375 degrees for 40 minutes.

Apples should be soft and the top brown and crisp.

Serve with vanilla ice cream or, as my dad likes it, a big chunk of old cheddar cheese!

Stocking Your Kitchen and China Cabinet for Hosting

Another sometimes tricky part of having a large family and hosting things like small group and potlucks is needing plenty of dishes and serving items for everyone! After all, we can't use paper plates for every meal. (At least that's what the environmentalists tell me. I'm kidding. I know we need to do a better job looking after the planet God gave us.)

Dean and I didn't register for anything when we got married. We were young and didn't fully understand the concept. We thought it meant we were being selfish and asking for things. We totally understood the benefits after the fact, when we had to buy wedding gifts for our friends, and their registries made it so much easier! Anyway, because we didn't register, our wedding gifts were a wonderful hodgepodge of things that our friends and family wanted to give us. There were no matching dishes, fancy china, or flatware, which meant that we didn't have to worry about offending anyone by replacing things or finding matching pieces for when our family grew and we started hosting more often. (We do have my grandmother's gold-rimmed white bone china now, but it gets used very infrequently because it's hand-wash only, and Momma ain't got time for that!)

Several years ago, conveniently around the same time our small mismatched wedding dish collection had begun to dwindle, a friend surprised me with a gift card to the mall for my birthday. But instead of buying clothes like I'm sure she thought I would, and probably needed to do at the time, I bought a boxed set of white dinnerware that was on sale! Surprise! It was to this simple set that I have added over the last several years by purchasing individual white plates, bowls, and mugs from kitchenware stores that sell dinnerware by the piece rather than by the set. I also pick up white pieces from Homesense and other similar stores when I see something we need . . . like more Rae Dunn mugs. (I joke. My kids would kill me if I bought another RD mug.) I've even purchased plenty of plain wine glasses at the dollar store and clear water glasses at Ikea for less than $1 each. They all go just fine with our white dishes. (They even appear beside the fine china on occasion. The horror.) And I don't worry about things getting broken because I know an entire set isn't ruined . . . just one little piece that can be replaced easily.

What and How Much Do You Need?

There are quite simply some things that will make hospitality easier for you if you keep them on hand. And multiples of some things will certainly make hosting easier too. So, here's a checklist of sorts to help you gather what you need without going overboard. It's sort of like my Decor Staples Checklist, but for hospitality. If you regularly host more people, increase the numbers listed below to match that. For example, we have our entire small group over every month. That's fifteen people! And if Dean's large family visits, that's a lot more! (Thus all the white plates stacked on our open kitchen shelves.)

Here are the basics:

- 12 dinner plates
- 12 lunch plates
- 12 side/salad/dessert-sized plates
- 12 salad/soup bowls
- 12 water glasses
- 12 sets of flatware (forks, spoons, knives)
- 6–12 wine glasses
- One set of nested mixing bowls
- Two serving platters (one large, one smaller)
- Two serving bowls (white casserole dishes can double up here if needed)
- A set of serving utensils (2–3 large spoons, a meat fork, and salad servers)
- One water pitcher
- One 8" square baking dish
- One 9" x 13" baking dish
- A set of pots and pans (at minimum a stock pot, sauté pan, and a sauce pan)
- Steak knives
- BBQ utensils
- Cooking utensils (spatula, slotted spoon, soup ladle, whisk, peeler, paring knife, serrated knife, and a chef's knife)
- One set of measuring cups and spoons
- Optional: ice bucket and tongs, cake stand, ramekins (we use these for snack dishes), divided appetizer dish, tiered tray, appetizer forks and spoons, gravy boat, garlic press, napkins, tablecloth, table runner, and napkin rings.

If you do not have these things already, and you're on a tight budget, look around at second-hand stores or yard sales. You can often find brand-new, still-in-the-box pieces to add to your kitchen necessities. And if you keep your dishware simple, you can either add to the dishes you have, or collect pieces over time, like I have. (And if you have to use paper plates in the meantime, I promise, I won't tell.)

How to Layer a Table Setting the Easy Way

Setting a pretty table for guests can be a special way to show you care about them. Of course, setting a pretty table isn't a necessity. You can keep things as simple as you'd like, and sometimes simple is best. But occasionally I do like to show our guests a little extra love with a pretty table by layering items I've collected when they were on sale or clearance (at Pier 1 and Homesense mostly).

Here's how I layer a table:

Clear everything off and give the table a good wipe down. I can't tell you the number of times I've forgotten to do this and been embarrassed at the crumbs in the cracks after I've set the whole thing!

Decide whether you want to use a tablecloth, table runner, or just placemats (or a combination). Put your choice(s) down on the table.

Now add a charger plate to each place, if you'd like. (A charger plate is a large decorative base setting on top of which you add the plates and other dinnerware.)

Add a dinner plate to each charger.

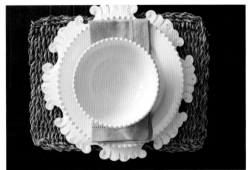

5 Place a rectangular folded napkin on the center of the plate (up and down, not side to side). If you want to make your own, I've got a tutorial for you at the end of the chapter!

6 Add another smaller plate or a bowl (if you will be having soup or salad).

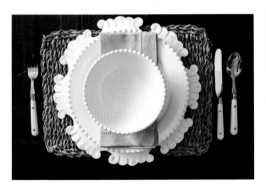

7 Then add your flatware. At the very least include a fork on the left and a knife and spoon on the right.

8 Then add a few candles or some flowers to the center of the table as a centerpiece.

Voilà! A pretty but simple table in about ten minutes.

DIY CLOTH NAPKINS

Pretty cotton napkins can be such a lovely addition to a table setting. Here's how to make your own to save money and choose whatever fabric you like.

SUPPLIES

- Two yards/meters of cotton fabric—washed, dried, and ironed
- Measuring tape
- Scissors
- Sewing machine
- Thread
- Straight pins
- Iron
- Ironing board

STANDARD NAPKIN SIZES

- Cocktail Napkin—6″ x 6″
- Hors d'Oeuvres Napkin—13″ x 13″
- Lunch Napkin #1—18″ x 18″
- Lunch Napkin #2—20″ x 20″
- Dinner Napkin #1—22″ x 22″
- Dinner Napkin #2—24″ x 24″
- Buffet Napkin (to be folded on lap)—27″ x 27″

INSTRUCTIONS

1. Decide on napkin size. Then cut your fabric to size, plus one inch on each side. For example, if you choose to make 24″ x 24″ dinner napkins, you would need to cut the fabric for each napkin to 26″ x 26″. (See standard napkin sizing list.)

2. With the cut napkin facedown, fold and iron the corners in.

3. Now fold in and iron about half an inch all the way around.

4. Repeat with a second fold of approximately half an inch, making the corners meet all neat and tidy. Pin all four corners.

5. Trim off the little piece of excess fabric.

6. Using a sewing machine, sew around the napkin near the outside edge and then again near the inside edge of the hem.

CONCLUSION

WELL, BEAUTIFUL, IN A way this is the end. But really, it's more of a beginning.

You now have all the tools and know-how that you need to make your home truly lovely. To make it the space you look forward to waking up to each and every day. To make it your happy place with God and your family at its center.

You've walked through and asked God to bless it and clear out the negative things. You're practicing an attitude of gratitude for the home you have, even if it's not your forever home. You know to whom your home belongs.

You've got a plan for decorating the whole place, and if you followed the steps in chapters 7, 8, and 9 as you read them, at least one room is decorated. You can complete the rest of the rooms at your pace, as time and budget allow, simply by repeating those steps.

You know what lovely hospitality looks like and how to practice it well so that you don't have to feel stressed-out inviting people in. You know how important it is to share your table with family and others.

Before I go, though, I want to remind you that just as there are seasons in the year, there are seasons of life.

When my children were small, our home looked very different than it does now. There were a lot fewer pretty things and a lot more primary colors . . . in the form of toys strewn everywhere. In fact, when I was writing this note to you, Facebook reminded me of this in the form of a photo memory I shared in 2013. The photo was of the side of our bathtub littered with bath toys. I had noted even then that I would miss that stage once it was gone. And sure enough, it was finished not long afterward.

I want to encourage you, if you are in a season of having young children at home, or one of living on an extra-tight budget, you can still have a lovely home. It may not look *exactly* as you'd like right now, but remember, it's not just about how your home looks. It's about creating a comfortable, peace-filled space. And practicing an attitude of gratitude for what it is.

What you focus on grows—in your mind at least—so focus on the good things about your home. Be thankful for the roof over your head and the people under that roof.

Also, dear beautiful one, I implore you *not to expect your home or the rooms in it to look like those you see in magazines.* Magazine homes don't even look like their photos, much like super models don't look entirely like their photos. They're Photoshopped to eliminate cords, dust bunnies, and other random things. They're meant to be beautiful to look at, but they're not a reflection of real life. It's amazing what camera angles and photography software can do. Trust me, as a designer and photographer, I know these things.

Our homes are meant to be lived in. Real life happens. Walls attract fingerprints that need to be cleaned. Pillows will get strewn about the living room. And the kitchen will become messy every single day, *if you're doing life right.* Embrace the mess. Embrace the imperfection. Embrace this most important place on earth.

Until we meet again . . .

xo, Shannon

ACKNOWLEDGMENTS

I HAD NO IDEA HOW HARD THIS was to do, until I sat down to do it. But I genuinely want to thank a few people for their practical help, guidance, and encouragement while I wrote this book.

Thank you to all of you who follow my blog and social media accounts and who sign up for my emails. Honestly, if you didn't keep coming back, this book wouldn't exist. Period.

Thank you to my first literary agent, Ruth Samsel. You were my first exposure to this book publishing world, and I couldn't have had anyone better to walk with me and get me started in the process. You helped to shape this book with your ideas, especially the one about making my first book all about what my "shtick" is.

Thank you to my second literary agent, Teresa Evenson, who took over when Ruth moved on to other things. I thank you for making that transition so smooth (even though I was terrified initially). You were the perfect person to walk me through waiting "forever" for responses from publishers and then negotiating my book deal. I appreciate you so much.

Thank you, Bethany House and Jennifer Dukes Lee. Thank you for taking a chance on me. Thank you, Jennifer, for being my champion right from the moment you saw my book proposal. For taking my book outline to those big important meetings and seeing the potential in what it could be. For encouraging me through the writing process. And praying for me through it all too. You are awesome!

For everyone who worked on the book design and layout. Thank you, William, for making my vision for the book's layout come to life. Thank you, Ellen, for making my words flow. Thank you, Kate, for coordinating the endorsements. You are a wonderful team to work with. Thank you for letting me in on the whole process.

Thank you to all my friends and family. For Beth & Chip, Tracey & Marty, Andy & Lisa, and other friends who prayed for me and celebrated with me. For those who took care of my kids for the day more than once. For Alex & Adam, who took the kids for a week in the midst of a busy season of their own so I could finish writing uninterrupted. For Dannyelle, who spent an entire summer's day helping me while I shot photos. For those who proofread certain chapters for accuracy and theological soundness. I appreciate you more than you know.

Thank you to my kids, Jonah, Lilly, and Meg. You put up with a lot of momma complaints while I asked you to "shhh" again so I could proofread. And you cleaned the house better than any cleaning lady could when I needed to get it ready for photos. You guys are growing into amazing young adults. I love you to the moon and back!

Thank you to my hubby, Dean. You encouraged me and supported me. You took on so much around the house and pressed pause on your own things for months so I could write this. Thank you, my bashert. I am forever thankful that God sent you to me just when I needed you most and that He's kept us close for over two decades.

And last but not least, to my heavenly Father, who knows I'm thankful for His prompting and consistent help but loves it when I thank Him anyway. Thank you for my life, my family, and my home.

NOTES

Chapter 1: The Most Important Place on Earth

1. T. S. Eliot, *Four Quartets* (New York: Houghlin Mifflin Harcourt, 1943, 1971), 180.
2. Robert Wolgemuth, *The Most Important Place on Earth: What a Christian Home Looks Like and How to Build One* (Nashville: Thomas Nelson, 2006, 2016).
3. Chloe Taylor, "Aesthetics and Well-Being: How Interior Design Affects Your Happiness," *Psychology Tomorrow Magazine*, July 2, 2016, http://psychology tomorrowmagazine.com/aesthetics-and-well-being-how-interior-design-affects -your-happiness.
4. Wolgemuth, *The Most Important Place on Earth*, xix.

Chapter 2: Practice an (Ongoing) Attitude of Gratitude

1. Doug Stone, vocalist, "Little Houses," by Skip Ewing and Mickey Cates, re-leased October 1994.

Chapter 4: 7 Steps to Declutter and Organize Everything

1. Andrew Mellen, quoted by Sandeep Kashyap in "7 Daily Habits of Highly Organized People," *Medium*, April 3, 2018, https://medium.com/swlh/7-daily-habits -of-highly-organized-people-ef95bfb07fdb.

Chapter 10: Lovely Hospitality

1. Amanda Wawryk, "Do you eat alone? Survey finds a lot of Canadians do," City-news 1130, June 18, 2018, www.citynews1130.com/2018/06/18/eat-alone-survey -finds-lot-canadians.
2. Martha Stewart, *Entertaining* (New York: Clarkson Potter, 1982), 15.
3. Dustin Willis and Brandon Clements, *The Simplest Way to Change the World* (Chicago: Moody, 2017), 26.
4. Willis and Clements, *The Simplest Way to Change the World*, 82–3.
5. Jen Schmidt, *Just Open the Door* (Nashville: B&H Books, 2018).
6. Father Jack King, quoted in Kevin Jesmer, "Why Scruffy Hospitality Creates Space for Friendship. Jack King / May 21, 2014," *Christian Family on Christ's Mission*, January 25, 2016, http://christianfamilyonchristsmission.com/why-scruffy-hospital ity-creates-space-for-friendship-jack-king-may-21-2014.

SHANNON ACHESON is a mostly self-taught designer, decorator, writer, and stylist. Although she has an interior design diploma, she'd much rather teach you how to decorate your own home than do it for you. (If you teach someone to fish, and all that.) She is the editor and designer behind the design and lifestyle company Home Made Lovely. Shannon resides in the suburbs of Toronto, Ontario, with her husband, Dean, their three homeschooled teenagers, and one little doggie named Jackson.